Yes! We'll Gather at the River!

Library of Congress Cataloging-in-Publication Data

Crafton, Barbara Cawthorne.
    Yes! We'll gather at the river! / Barbara Cawthorne Crafton.
        p. cm. — (JourneyBook)
    ISBN 0-89869-332-2 (pbk.)
    1. Christian life—Anglican authors.   I. Title. II. Series.
    BV4510.3 .C73 2001
    248.4′83—dc21

                                2001028154

JourneyBook and colophon are registered trademarks of Church Publishing Incorporated.

Church Publishing Incorporated
445 Fifth Avenue
New York, NY 10016

www.churchpublishing.org

5 4 3 2 1

Yes! We'll Gather at the River!

Barbara Cawthorne Crafton

A
JourneyBook ™
from
Church Publishing Incorporated New York

To some dear ones:

to John Gorga, 1923–1998,
and Bertha, his wife,
who still remembers
"Let me call you 'Sweetheart'";
and most of all
to Thomas Lee Winston, 1941–2001;
the world will not see his like again.

Far too many people did far too many things in bringing this little book into the world for me to name them all. We'll just do categories: the editorial team at Church Publishing, especially Johnny Ross and Joan Castagnone; the people of St. Clement's Church in sunny Hell's Kitchen, NYC; the People of the Pickle; the Finger Lakes Conference; the Kenyon Conference; Trinity Church in the City of New York; the Society of St. Francis; the Episcopal Writers' Colony; the Community of the Holy Spirit; and, most of all, my family.

Blessings on them all.

"I HOPE WHITE TURBAN IS THERE TODAY," my husband said as we soared into the sky. We were riding the Roosevelt Island tram over the East River. White Turban is a majestic black woman who lives at Goldwater Hospital, a woman with an exquisite gospel voice, and Q, my husband, loved her. Before coming to St. Clement's, where I am the only priest and therefore must be present every Sunday, I used to fill in for Brother Derek at Goldwater Hospital when he needed to be away. Goldwater is on Roosevelt Island, in the East River, which separates Manhattan from Queens. You could reach it by car, but we preferred to take the tram, a conveyance somewhat like a ski lift, which sails up into the air and out over the river on thin cables before settling gently into its cradle on the other side. You walked across the island to Goldwater, a sprawl of masonry standing right next to the gothic ruins of the old TB sanatorium—with its empty, arched windows showing sky through them—where nineteenth-century consumptives languished within sight of Manhattan but closed away from it forever.

Goldwater was a little like that. It was a city hospital for the chronically ill, the hospital of last resort for those whose intractable diseases and small purses precluded their placement anywhere else. Paralysis, profound mental retardation, cerebral palsy, multiple sclerosis, stroke, gunshot—any one of a number of things could land a person in Goldwater for the rest of her life.

. . . . .

The interior of the hospital was tiled a weary green, like a forties-style bathroom. We walked from wing to wing to wing along an endless central corridor, down which the nurses strode and the patients wheeled slowly along—some sitting, some lying on gurneys, some motorized, almost none under his own steam. Along the main corridor walls were affixed brave bulletin boards: boards honoring volunteers; boards announcing professional seminars for hospital staff; boards displaying the art-work and writing of patients (drawings of voluptuous dream women, pictures of Christmas trees, longing poems about wives and children, real and imaginary); boards listing patients' birthdays.

At the very end of the corridor were the chapels. I was always impressed by how large and pleasant they were, remarkable in a city hospital. Somebody involved in the architecture must have gotten religion. And whoever it was also got ecumenism: there are three of them, Catholic, Jewish, and Protestant, side by side. We were at the far end of the wing.

We entered and turned on the lights. The Blessed Mother's candle had gone out again, so I lit it, illuminating her face so we could all see who she was. My husband found the list of patients who wanted to come to church, and went off to begin fetching them. Meanwhile, I got to work preparing the altar for the Eucharist. The chapel was airy and light, with polished floors and light wooden paneling and a wall of large windows on one side. There was an altar and a lectern and a prie-dieu. Although there were a few chairs along the perimeter of the room, most of the floor was empty. These worshipers brought their own chairs.

· · · · ·

They were starting to arrive. A grandmotherly lady first, beautifully dressed for church in a dark navy dress and a hat, pushing her own wheelchair slowly in front of her. Her large black purse rode in the chair. Finding a spot by the window, she settled carefully into the chair and began to examine the service leaflet. My husband was back with a man in a wheelchair, and a woman on a gurney waited in the hall for him to steer her through the chapel door. Mr. Waters entered in his chair, sailing purposefully toward the front of the chapel and then wheeling around to face the door. Before his accident, he had been a Pentecostal minister; paralyzed, now, from the waist down, he still liked to be up front. With him were his wife and little boy, who came faithfully each Sunday to attend church with him. She was young and very beautiful, but I never saw her smile.

My husband was really moving now, appearing and reappearing with more people in wheelchairs. And here was Alonzo. Slowly, slowly Alonzo worked his chair over to the lady in the navy dress, a special friend of his. His tongue protruded permanently from his immobile face. His legs were immobile, too, and wasted. His hands were stiff as boards: he had no oppositional movement in either of them, so he could not grasp anything. This handicapped him greatly in his current project, which was to retrieve the service leaflet his friend had dropped on the floor. Fighting my increasingly urgent longing to do it for him, I tried not to watch as he made sweep after sweep with his rigid hands. Finally he succeeded in catching the thin paper against the side of his chair and slowly bringing it up along the leg until his friend could take it from him. I realized that I had been holding my breath. The

· · · · ·

grandmotherly lady smiled and patted his hand. He gazed at her in what seemed to me to be love. Why I thought that I cannot say: Alonzo's face is paralyzed. He cannot show his emotions in his face.

A youngish woman with MS arrived in her motorized chair. She had loved Vespers at St. Thomas on Fifth Avenue, she once told me; she used to go every Sunday evening when she was in better health and still lived in Manhattan. Her eyes were quick and sharp, but everything else about her body was painfully slow; hands, speech.

And now here at last was White Turban, sure and steady in her chair as she glided in the door and toward the window to sit beside her friend in the navy dress. White Turban dressed completely in white every Sunday. She had come to the hospital years ago—1959?—after having fallen from the roof of her apartment building to the fifth floor. This story intrigued me. How does one fall from the roof to the fifth floor and stop there? Why did she fall? Was she pushed? These wonderings I kept to myself, and White Turban was not forthcoming with further details.

It was time for the service to begin. The chapel was now full of wheelchairs and gurneys: thirty-five or so in attendance that day. We sang an "opening" hymn—you couldn't really call it a "processional," since nobody was in any position to walk anywhere. It was an Episcopal Eucharist, even though the attendees came from the whole neighborhood of American Protestantism. I did not have to solo on the prayers and hymns, though: they all sang them, or hummed along if they did not know the words. At communion, I moved around the chapel from chair to chair to

· · · · ·

chair: everybody at Goldwater intincted, since sipping from a cup was so hard for so many of them and there was just something odd about receiving the wine through a straw. I dipped each wafer into the chalice and placed it on a person's tongue: White Turban, the St. Thomas lady, the Rev. Mr. Waters, my husband, Alonzo—whose tongue was as motionless as the rest of him—his dear friend in the navy dress. And Cathy, who lay on her gurney in the middle of the crowd. She had lived in the hospital since she was six, and she was sixty-five when I first met her. A cerebral palsy patient like Alonzo, she was not as motionless, but the movements of her hands and face were not of her authoring. I pictured her on her first night there all those years ago, tiny in her new strange bed in a ward full of strangers, huddled under the bleach-smelling sheets, longing for her mother. She told Brother Justus once that she felt God had been very good to her. Sometimes, though, she was overcome with sorrow, and wept.

My sermon was going to be about patience, but it deserted me when I stood to preach. Instead, I began to talk about *them*. They were the ones, I told them, who knew the most about what it is to long for something. They were the ones who knew what it is to be weak, and they were also the ones who knew that physical weakness is not the final word that able-bodied people think it is. They were the ones whom God loved most tenderly. They were the ones whose lives had trained them and strengthened them for eternal life. Many modern people feel uncomfortable with talk of heaven, but not this group. They were ready to go.

When the Eucharist was finished, we had another hymn. It was "Shall we gath-

· · · · ·

er at the river." Everyone knew it, and everyone sang, a strange cacophonous mix of sounds and tunes and tunelessness. The Rev. Mr. Waters was in his element, and so was White Turban, her rich, low voice leading all the singing. Many of the people could not clap their hands, but they banged their fists weakly on the arms of their chairs on every *Yes!*

> *Yes, we'll gather at the river,*
> *The beautiful, the beautiful river;*
> *Gather with the saints at the river*
> *That flows by the throne of God.*

The service was finished, and all the people had been wheeled back. My husband and I walked back across the island, away from the gray of Goldwater's exterior and the old sanatorium silhouetted against the blue sky. We were in luck: the tram was right there.

Somehow I thought that the people from Goldwater Hospital were coming, too. I thought that they were right behind us. I thought that they were running along the grass, skipping, leaping with their straight, strong legs. I thought that they were holding hands and laughing and singing, and I thought that there was not a wheelchair or a gurney in sight, no, not a single one. I thought that they all piled into the Roosevelt Island tram with us, and that we were lifted up, up, high over the East River with its swirling, dangerous currents. The beautiful river. That flows by the throne of God.

. . . . .

I LOOK AT MY WATCH: 1:30 in the afternoon on Thanksgiving Day. I send a grand-daughter on a reconnaissance run into the dining room. Is the table clear yet? She bounces back into the kitchen and announces that it most certainly is not. "Far from it," says her sister. We all roll our eyes heavenward.

The dining table is one part of my husband's filing system. The kitchen table is another: both are covered with papers. The kitchen counter, already awkwardly placed and hard to work on, also is covered with papers. The coffee table in the living room is covered. So are fifty percent of the available chair seats and one of the two couches.

Sometimes I feel that I am drowning in papers. No, not drowning: I am being walled up in them, as if the piles were coming closer to me, closing in on me. Sometimes I feel that I am like the man in the Poe story "The Cask of Amontillado": *For the love of God, Montresor!*

We won't be able to set the table until the piles are gone. My snowy damask tablecloth and crisp napkins, my mother's silver and my grandmother's china, the candles, the ruby cranberry sauce in its crystal dish, the majestic turkey itself—all homeless until I have a table on which to put them.

"Are we going to serve it buffet style?" Rosie asks, smelling defeat.

"Never!" I snap. But I don't go out there myself to settle things. I don't find my spouse and scold him. I can't.

. . . . .

I know that he hates his piles of papers, too. I know that, for him, they are sins of omission, hard evidence of tasks that cry out to be finished, symbols of everything in his life that has been left undone. I know that he feels indicted by each of them. I know that he finds it hard to credit himself with any goodness as long as he is aware of any flaw. And so I hold back on my anger about the piles. I carefully avoid leaving piles of my own in clear view, staking my claim on a nice plot of moral high ground, so that the Golden Rule will come down on my side, should it be invoked.

But I am not always so saintly about the piles. I have exploded about them on occasion, noisily demanding their immediate eradication. I remember a particularly ugly scene in which I insisted that he pick up the bedroom that minute. He knelt down and began. I remained standing, keeping a stern watch on his progress. He filled about two bags before the sadomasochism of the project sickened us both. I never did that again, and I never will. But I have attacked them myself, an act that hits him like a boot to the solar plexus. The thought that I might invade the piles and perhaps even throw something out haunts him like a dream of death.

"I know where everything is," he says, and he does. Forty-five years of teaching have honed his filing technique to perfection. He can fish out a "Rise of the Novel" exam he gave in 1958, its lurid purple mimeograph ink still vivid against the faded mimeo paper; he can locate a particular edition of a particular book from a forest of identical book cartons. The filing system offends my longing for beauty and order, but even I must admit that it works.

. . . . .

"We have such a pretty house," I say. "I'd just like it to show. I'd like to have the use of a table."

Occasionally, a doctrine will be proclaimed. "Let's establish a distinction between public and private spaces," he says, "and no pile of paper will be allowed in the public ones." I enthusiastically agree. But doctrine is no match for human nature—never has been, in Church or World. The Doctrine of Public and Private Spaces has eroded quickly each time it has been promulgated. An encroaching deadline, an impending lecture: these urgencies shove their way into the dining room, into the kitchen, where they put their elbows on the table. I swallow my wrath again. I don't want to add being married to a shrew to Q's other burdens.

Our house is beautiful. It is 120 years old, and we have painted it many remarkable colors, inside and out, so many that it is famous in our town, and people wonder if its occupants might not be a bit off. Its furnishings are old and lovely. Lace curtains at the long dining room windows fall luxuriously in a trail of white against red walls onto shining floor. And almost every surface is covered with piles of paper, blue books, newspaper clippings, manila folders.

I arrive home one night before he does. This is unusual: I am always the late one, and I always come up the walk and catch a glimpse of him reading in his chair, bathed in the golden light of the lamp at his elbow. Not tonight: the house is dark and seems larger than usual. No porch light is on. I let myself in the front door and put on the light in the window so that he will see it when he comes in. I start upstairs. I get ready for bed and turn on the radio. I always play the radio when I

· · · · ·

am home alone, but tonight, the music seems intrusive. I turn it off and roll over on my side, facing the other side of the bed. His side.

Someday, this is what it will be like. Home to a silent house with no lights on. Getting into bed all alone. The bed is old. It is too old to accommodate a standard modern mattress, and so we must travel many miles to an obscure shop that re-stuffs custom mattresses. It needs re-stuffing every five years or so. But our bodies make their marks within a few months: two oval depressions with a ridge in between. Now I lie in my trough and look at his empty one. This is what it will be like someday.

Except that there will be no piles. Not in this bedroom, nor on the dining room table, nor on the kitchen table. I will have taken all the books back to the Rutgers library and canceled all the eighteenth-century journal subscriptions. The scraps of paper with phone numbers on them will be tossed, along with the blue books and the newspaper clippings.

Or maybe that is not what I will do. Maybe I will take all the papers and make a pile of them on the bed, in the trough next to mine. They will be substantial; paper in stacks is heavy. Maybe they will feel substantial at night, and maybe I can lean against the pile as I now lean against him, and maybe it will be as if he were still here.

. . . . .

"I JUST HOPE the gay and lesbian group doesn't ever get, you know, political," a young woman tells me. She loves St. Chad's; is proud that it is sufficiently broad-minded to have a gay and lesbian group; likes to attend the group's social events, the parties and get-togethers it sponsors, even though she herself is straight. She may feel entitled to a secret congratulation, too, for her own broad-mindedness. She begins to feel uncomfortable, though, when some members of the group talk about advocacy.

"Can't it be a *way into* St. Chad's, she asks, "You know, like a young mothers' group?" It seems self-evident to her that a group expressing itself about issues will not be a way into a warm and loving community. That to focus any attention on painful truths would be to foreclose on the integrated congregation she loves. And so the gay dinner parties are fine. Just nothing political.

She loves her church. She is a little surprised to have come to a faith that matters profoundly to her in her forties after a life that has never given the matter much thought. She and a lot of other people. We might call it a spiritual boom. Everyone loves angels these days: those hybrid agents/lawyers/personal shoppers who fly to earth once in a while to pay off our credit card debt and get us out of any other messes into which we've wandered. Everyone wants to learn to meditate and visualize. Labyrinths have sprung up in church halls and gardens across America like kudzu, and half the books on *The New York Times* bestseller list are about spirituality. A year or two ago, the "Travel Section" contained an article comparing the culinary styles and accommodations of a dozen monasteries as if they were contenders for Michelin stars. Prayer lowers your blood pressure, we read, and actual tests have shown that gall bladder patients for whom people are praying get better faster than those who go it alone. So spirituality is good for you, like vitamins.

Nothing wrong with lower blood pressure. And who doesn't want gall bladder patients to improve rapidly? I do. But it ought not to surprise us that the current spirituality boom is as self-absorbed as everything else in our era. Why wouldn't it be? It is a far cry from the self-giving discipline to which we are heir, and we ought not to rejoice too wholeheartedly at its domestication. "Good for you" is just not good enough. "Makes me happy" is wonderful, but there is more to spiritual integrity than a hug and a smile. In the end, the spiritual life prepares the people of God for a holy life and a holy death, not for a more sublime form of egotism.

In particular, let's not use personal spirituality to support or excuse ethical and moral passivity. Prayer and sacrament are not a way out of dealing with a suffering world, nor do they absolve any of us from the human responsibility to work to end suffering. It is a cheap spirituality that encourages the believer to start and stop with her own personal fulfillment, as if Christian spirituality were not about a God who laid down the gift of life for us, who has empowered some so profoundly that they could surrender their lives willingly and even joyfully. We venerate the martyrs, and not for their good blood pressure. To domesticate the spiritual life, encouraging the

· · · · ·

people of God to think that the search for the true, healthy self is the end of the Christian journey instead of what it is—the beginning—is to regard our personal relationship with God through prayer and sacrament as instrumentally "useful." It is not useful. It is central. It is why God made us.

And, as we consider the domestication of the spiritual life, a more sinister idea takes shape, in the form of the ancient lawyer's question: *Qui bono?* Who will benefit? The history of the relation between Church and State has rarely been an inspiring one: Marx considered religion the opiate of the people for a reason. If those whose faith might propel them into advocacy can be convinced that this is not their ministry, that they must choose between it and a fulfilling life of prayer, then the forces of oppression can pursue their terrible work with one less obstacle. Why all the angel books and movies? Because they make money. And with money comes power, the power to get money and keep money and get more money. In our world, that power needs the poor to stay poor: the only way to make the poor richer would be for the rich to become poorer, and that is not on the table. The fact that an individual within the moneyed power structure may be unaware of this need and his relationship to it—and may give to charity and pray earnestly for the suffering—does not mean he's not participating in an oppressive economy. If we are involved with the economy at all—and we all are—then we live within its rules. If it is in our economic interest to understand our walk with Christ to be strictly a private affair, we will not see that our self-absorbed lives continue to be lived on the backs of the poor. We will not see that our lives collude with an oppressive

. . . . .

system, even if our lives are now "spiritual." I used to buy cocktail dresses; now I buy Jesus books. But my buying and selling are economically exactly what they were before. God does not call us closer in the mystical encounter for ourselves alone.

Such cynicism! I thought this was supposed to be a devotional book.

We are tired, and afraid of conflict. In the fifties, we tell ourselves, everyone went to church, and today just about nobody does. We look at the decade that followed and blame it: it was the sixties' emphasis on social justice that drove people away, we say, and so the people of faith have turned from ministries of advocacy in favor of ministries of spirituality. Thank God we're finally focusing on theology, we say, as if the mighty compassion of God had not strode through the Old Testament over-turning tyranny and wrong and calling the chosen to make that righteousness the sign of their faith. You don't get people into churches by scolding them, we say—and you certainly don't. But is calling the people of God to reflect more faithfully the image of God always scolding? Are we ever allowed to hope for justice and to pray for it, or is it rude now even to bring it up? If we understand personal spiri-tuality to be a crowd pleaser and sell it so our churches will grow and prosper (soft-pedaling the whole truth about what the cost of discipleship might be), we embody only a part of who Christ is. Christ is not only here to make our individual lives better. He is here to redeem the world from sin and death in all their forms, public and private. The life of faith can never be just about me. There is always an us.

For Christ's sake, question the supposed gulf between spirituality and activism.

. . . . .

Believing in that gulf and acting on that belief has not been helpful to us. It has made us caricature one another, stereotyping our sisters and brothers in a way that, in the end, stereotypes us. We think there are two kinds of people: spiritual people who deeply suspect politics, and activists who have no time for the mystical journey and regard it as a craven excuse not to engage a righteous cause. We think that there are people who peddle pie-in-the-sky-when-you-die, and other people who have deified their own political agendas; people of prayer, and people of action. We conduct ourselves as if we believed this, and eagerly sort ourselves into one or the other camp. In that sorting, we make the Solomonic choice to cut ourselves in half.

But there aren't people called to be spiritual and other people called to be political. We all are called to a closer walk with the God who loves us and longs for us to love back. And we, by nature, are political animals. Why do we have such confidence in an anthropology that cuts human beings in two? Why is it so acceptable in church circles, and why is it such wicked fun, to be so dismissive of one another over this? "I don't know anything about *spirituality*," the college chaplain tells me impatiently. Derision drips from the word. The chaplain's work with young people revolves around political advocacy: they go to demonstrations and get arrested. They are strong neighborhood activists. But when a chaplaincy colleague at the same college talks with students about prayer and life, and plans retreats, the first chaplain can scarcely be bothered to attend. One is training Christian activists. The other is practicing the care of souls.

Life would be a great deal simpler if this false dichotomy were true. But life is

. . . . .

not simple. The fully integrated soul is still a restless soul, for there is evil in the world, and we oppose it. The desire to retain and expand power remains in the holiest of us, and we oppose it within ourselves in the rigorous and painful honesty prayer demands.

St. Athanasius spent his life describing the nature of the Incarnation—not a cool intellectual enterprise in his day: people killed each other over whether or not the Holy Spirit proceeded from the Father *and* the Son. We remember him for this phrase: "God became mortal that mortals might become God." Scandalous! Do we really dare to say that we hope to become God? But that is exactly our hope: that we are and will be part of the complete unity that is God. We have mythologized this reality as "heaven" where—St. Paul tells us—"we will be in Christ and Christ will be all in all." No division, within us or among us. A long way from our current experience. But, even here, even within this tumultuous current experience, we don't have to settle for a divided life in a divided family.

THIS WAS JUST A DREAM.

My father was still alive and married to my stepmother, but my mother was there, too. All three of them were there. Somehow, in the dream, my mother was no longer dead, but uncomfortably present in the midst of my dad's new life. There she sat in her old bathrobe, her back straight, her shoulders motionless, her eyes downcast to hide her hurt at being replaced. I was darting frantically from room to room, attempting to explain the situation. "She's not dead anymore," I said helplessly to my father. "I don't know how this is so, but it is so." From my mother, I tried to hide the fact that I loved my stepmother. My mother remained silent. It seemed that she knew she was in the wrong place. My father and his new wife went about their homely business—I think they were doing the dishes together. They could not see my mother. But she could see them. How cruel it was.

At length, she looked at me and said, "I won't be back." She began to grow transparent, and I watched her fade from sight. I knew she would not come to me that way again. I awoke, glad that it was not real. But it was a terrible thing, that she no longer belonged in our life.

It was the true, though. Life goes on without the beloved dead. It closes up without so much as a ripple over the place where they were. "Here is no abiding city," St. Augustine said. One by one, we all fade away. At first, it seems impossible. In time, it becomes just another sad fact. And, eventually, some of the sadness even fades away, and it is just a fact: they are gone.

Augustine lived and wrote in the declining years of the Roman Empire, at the time of the sack of Rome, which seemed to people in those days like the very end of the world. He imagined the world as like the Eternal City, and it was revealed to be anything but eternal. That person, that institution—all those whose absence is unthinkable to us will one day be gone. That which we cannot live without—we *will* live without one day.

And when that happens, we will know something new about ourselves. That within each loss is an emancipation of sorts, a slow and painful relaxation of our desperate grip on the things we love and count on to remain. They do not remain, and we go on. And then we do not remain, and the world goes on. And then the world will not remain, and God will go on.

Will You Be Faithful?
· · · · ·

I LOVE THE DAILY OFFICE, that comforting cycle of morning, noonday, evening, and nighttime prayer with which Christians have embraced their days for more than a thousand years. I loved saying it in seminary, all of us together in the beautiful chapel there, loved hearing the haunting beginning of the *Phos hilaron* in the evening: "O-O-O gracious light . . ."; the syllables lingering and stretching themselves out exquisitely on the cantor's melody, a tune that sounded ancient but was composed by an alumnus only a few years ahead of me. The rest of us joined in sweetly, sweeter far than we really were: "cle-ar brightness of the everlasting Father in he-a-ven. . . ."

All my life, people I have admired have been faithful in this daily round of prayer: my father, the rector of my first church, so many colleagues I respected so much. People throughout the ages have said and sung these words, and when I say or sing them, I am one with all those people. Faithful, as they were. And joyous in my faithfulness: the framework of the Office holds each day in a sweet and homely basket. I might awaken and build a fire, so I can say Morning Prayer by its flickering light, and then I will dress and go out into my world fortified and calm. Or draw a lovely hot bath with lavender, and say Morning Prayer stretched out in it, the fragrant water soaking my aching bones and muscles with warmth. My Prayer Book looks as if someone has cried all over Morning Prayer, but it's just the lavender water. I am

· · · · ·

hoping that a sweet smell of lavender wafts from it after my death, and I will be made a saint.

I have tucked myself in with Compline and fallen gently to sleep, serene and at peace. There is nothing about this routine that is not lovely.

So isn't it odd that, for years, a daily practice that gave me so much positive reinforcement always broke down? One week, two weeks, three weeks of consistent daily prayer with all the satisfactions it always brings. But then I would have a breakfast meeting and arise too late for Morning Prayer. So I would make up for it that evening by doing all the readings, the ones for morning and the ones for evening as well. And then I'd miss an evening and be too tired to make it up at Compline. Before I knew it, I had run up quite a tab of missed mornings and evenings, and I would no longer bother to make them up. And then, like a dieter who succumbs to temptation in the morning and therefore sees no reason not to eat a cake in the afternoon, I would allow the Daily Office to slip away. A failure, again.

It wasn't that I thought it was sinful not to say the Daily Office. I knew God loved me whether or not I said Morning Prayer. I just wanted to be faithful, wanted that holy rhythm to support my strenuous days. I loved the way my life felt when I was true to it. I felt discouraged and more than a little fraudulent that I, a religious leader looked to by many for guidance, a writer of devotional books and articles, a spiritual director who had helped dozens of people make the regular round of daily prayer a dependable part of their lives, to their deep and abiding joy, seemed unable to do it myself. Why could I not make myself one of those people whose faithfulness I so admired?

That was before I realized something profound—be frightened when writer describes her own insight as "profound"—and yet so simple that I cannot now understand how I could have missed it: Prayer is not a job. It's a gift.

May I repeat myself? Prayer is not a job. It's a gift.

Prayer is not something I work myself to death to create as a gift to God. Prayer is something God gives to me. The God who created us loves us, and longs for us to be in touch. Prayer is not something I do for God, one more way for me to be Miss Perfect and earn my way into the divine favor. My inflexible focus on my consistency, my perfect attendance obscured my vision of what is really going on in prayer: God is reaching out to me and longs for me to respond. So I don't have to *make* my prayer discipline. All I have to do is ask for it. That's all anyone has to do.

What made me grasp this? I haven't a clue. Despair, maybe, the clear sense of having failed. But I asked for the gift of prayer that was best for me at that time, and God gave me that gift. For me, it *is* Morning and Evening Prayer. The occasional Compline. A rare Noonday. Nothing like the machine-like consistency I used to think I should have firmly in place. But accompanied, every time, with the certainty that I am connected with a loving God through a merciful Savior.

"Certainty?" asks a woman in the front row, who has been listening intently as I say all this at a workshop on prayer. "But that's my problem exactly. Do you mean you always feel an absolutely certain sense of God's presence when you pray? Half the time, I don't feel anything!" So I see that I've been standing up in front of a roomful of church people talking about my prayer life, and it has sounded like each occasion of prayer is a mountaintop moment. Oops. I didn't mean to give that impression. I don't have an intense emotional experience each time I pray. Sometimes I do. But sometimes I feel very little. And so it is very important for us to understand something: the quality or validity of prayer is not measured by our feelings. Feelings come and go. Prayer is a connection with God, who stays put. If you require a great rush of feelings to certify your prayer experience as valid or real, despair is very near you. Prayer doesn't need certification. It already *is* valid.

It seems to me that we, the legatees of the neo-Romanticism of the sixties, need to examine some of our assumptions. That decade—so influential in American religious self-understanding—assigned a high value to feelings and emotions, an ultimate value, in fact, beyond what human feelings can bear. Feelings certified everything. Marriages ended, parents deserted children, people gave up on half-started degrees and careers, all manner of commitments were abandoned like out-of-gas Chevys, all because the feeling was gone. We became a generation famous for its inability to delay even the smallest of gratifications.

Certainly feelings matter. Certainly they are human. Certainly they propel us in important directions, and certainly life would be a sterile exercise without them. But they are only part of what makes us human. They are not the whole of us. We are also intellect. And we are duty and conscience. All of these comprise us, and we are not fully ourselves if we lack any of them.

. . . . .

It's not that feelings are unimportant in the spiritual life. They are a great incentive. I merely point out that life is not just a set of feelings—a helpful thing to understand when nothing warm and fuzzy happens as you pray. Those times don't mean that God has abandoned you; God never abandons you. They don't mean your prayer is awful. They just mean you're not having a warm and fuzzy day. And so you pray from the emotional place you inhabit, which is not always the top of the world.

This is very good news for overscheduled people, who don't have long, quiet afternoons in which to get in the mood for prayer. It turns out that your mood doesn't matter, and you don't need to wait for the right one to settle over you like a soft blanket. You don't need to tell polite lies to God about how happy and grateful you are if, in fact, you're neither of those things. You can rely on the habit you have developed and the practice to which you have accustomed yourself to carry you in faith through times and experiences that your emotions, by themselves, could never sustain.

Theresa of Ávila was an overscheduled person if there ever was one. She traveled all over Europe, founded many monasteries, wrote a dozen or so books of ascetical theology (most of which are still in use today), and kept up a voluminous correspondence with the popes and monarchs of her time. She is the only woman in history to have been accorded the title "Doctor of the Church." It is said that she was approached by a young sister who was discouraged with her prayer life because she wasn't *feeling* much of anything—this to Teresa, whose famous Bernini ecstasy has

· · · · ·

titillated art history students for more than four hundred years. Teresa answered her reassuringly with a phrase I have found to be a life-saver more than once: "Sterile prayer pierces Heaven."

Sterile prayer pierces heaven. God knows our prayers, no matter what is or is not going on in our emotions. It's pretty easy to pray when praying makes us ecstatic. But God also knows that we get discouraged during our dry spells, that there is sometimes precious little in the way of emotional gratification in prayer, and so we can imagine that God is especially touched by our prayer at these times. "Look at that," God says, "she is reaching out to relate to me even though she's feeling dry and discouraged." And God loves the effort, the same way parents love the funny-looking artwork that travels home from kindergarten and ends up fastened with magnets to the refrigerator door. Not because it's great art, but because they dearly love the little hands that made it. Just so God loves our prayer—not because it creates a full and sufficient emotional experience every time, but because we show up even when it doesn't.

But there is more for us than God's kindly forbearance with our moods. There is more to be said about our feelings and emotions, and it is good news: the devotional habit you build, as effective as it is in carrying you through your sterile periods, will also assist in evoking the feelings for which we cannot help but long.

You recall the experiments of the Russian experimental psychologist Pavlov who, by ringing a bell each time a subject group of dogs were fed, conditioned them to salivate just at the sound of the bell. You may remember a similar phe-

. . . . .

nomenon in yourself from your own student days: I had a carrel in the library at seminary, where I kept my books and did my studying and writing. Day after day I worked there, always in the same place. After a time, just being there made me ready to work: the smell of the old books, the pressure of that particular chair against the small of my back, the feel of the desk's smooth wood, the hush of the stacks, broken only rarely by quiet footsteps or whispered conversations. Being there made me ready and eager.

Your prayer habit conditions your emotions in just the same way. Over time, being in the prayer place and doing the prayer things makes you feel like praying. This is one advantage of using at least some "canned" prayer and not relying exclusively on your own spontaneity. If you always begin with the Lord's Prayer, or the Prayer of St. Francis, or the *Gloria Patri*, or the Jesus Prayer or just about anything on a regular basis, it will come to trigger prayerfulness within you. You can squander a lot of heartbreak trying to drum up feelings to get you started and not achieve them. Maybe it's time to relax a little and let yourself be carried by something ancient and dependable to start with. A little conditioning can be a very good thing.

Priests promise that they will be "faithful in the prayers" when they are ordained. You may or may not have taken this vow, but *will* you? Will you be faithful? I certainly *do* will to be faithful, and count on God to help me be faithful and show me how. On my own, though, my will is insufficient, as is yours and everyone else's. But the news is good: God is with us. We are not on our own.

We are not, after all, in hot pursuit of a God who wishes to elude us. We are

. . . . .

reaching back to a God who has reached for us first, again and again and again. In the very act of praying at all—however rudimentary a prayer—you are in God's presence.

. . . . .

THE YOUNG WOMAN who has come for a visit is an extremely moral person, one who has demonstrated, many times, her willingness to put her money where her mouth is. You can count on her to raise a painful ethical issue when no one else will, and she will stay with it even when people roll their eyes and pretend to be bored (when they're really feeling just a wee bit guilty).

The intercessions bother her. "Do we really think that God will heal someone just because we mention her name, and won't bother if we don't?" She feels that something is a-kilter in singling out the people we know and love from a suffering world, as if the divine blessing were, like so much else in this world, basically a matter of who you know. As if God were not disposed to heal us at all, and must be wheedled into it by our cajoling prayers.

I get what she's saying. Prayer for the lives of others and for ourselves is a loaded topic, for what we think prayer is springs directly from what we think God is. Begin a discussion of prayer, and it can become a minefield a lot sooner than a person might think. We believe that God is active in human affairs. But not one of us knows just how that is so. Each of us is fiercely protective of his or her own theory of God's ways with us (in fact, much *more* protective than we are with any of our other theories), and we are apt to be a bit rough on people who think of God in ways different from ours. Sometimes a lot rough. Odd that the creator of the universe should seem so in need of a vigorous defense, but there it is.

So, what *are* we doing when we pray? Are we talking God into favors he would otherwise be indisposed to grant? Are we wielding magical powers, conjuring up a God who acts like a powerful but obedient genie? Or are we merely thinking kindly thoughts about those into whose lives misfortune has come, and hoping for the best?

Even people who do not believe in God—and most certainly do not pray—are sometimes very interested in precisely what those of us who *do* think we are doing. I am rehearsing a play. Another actor sidles up to me during a break and begins to talk about his ailing father. I ask for his dad's first name and say that I will pray for him, and that I will put his name on the congregation's prayer list as well. He tells me that he really doesn't believe in organized religion, and gives me a short history of the spiritual journey that has led to his current skepticism. But he finishes by telling me that the prayers mean a lot to him, and I believe him. A few months later, he writes me a long letter about his dad's peaceful death.

Perhaps he connects me with an earlier innocence of his own, a time when he still believed in a God who answers prayer. Perhaps he half believes that there *is* some magic he has left behind, a person or group of people somewhere who can order up miracles of healing as if they were pizzas. Whatever he believes, even if he believes me to be the befuddled curator of a hopelessly outdated way of life, he appreciates the prayers, and his father's name stays on the list until he dies.

To what end?

· · · · ·

For the record, I do not believe that God withholds healing from people until they pray the right way. I don't think God has to be talked into loving us—God already loves us. I don't believe that certain people have an inside track to the love of God unavailable to God's other children.

But I do know that, when we pray, we are adding our own love to the love of God. God's love for each of us is total and complete; nothing more is needed from us. But in praying for one another, we turn our hearts in the direction of another as God's heart is turned to her. We turn toward her in love. And love is *energy*, even the small love of which we are capable, energy like the immeasurable love of God is energy, the energy out of which God created the human race and everything else. Love causes us to exist, and we exist in the medium of love, as tiny one-celled animals exist in the medium of water, or in the medium of air. And when we become aware of the love within us, the love that caused and causes us to be, we stand as God stands and see what God sees. We are like a circuit breaker: we open ourselves, and the love of God flows through us. We don't *do* anything; we merely affirm what is already so: God loves us, and loves the one for whom we pray. We shine the light of our love on another, and the light of God's love shines on him, too. It must, for any love we have *is* God's love—we have no other source of love *except* God.

Pray for someone, and you are joined to that person in love. This is true whether or not you know the person—and even if you don't like her. The love of which we speak when we speak of prayer is not the ephemeral love of romantic emotion; it is the steady love of our decision to live in the medium of God's love. It is a love that knows the one for whom we pray to be beloved of God, a love that turns toward that sister or brother and speaks her name, his name, and knows that the heart of God is also turned toward her, toward him. I don't need to know these people for this to be true. I don't need to know them in order to turn God's heart toward them. God's heart is already turned toward them.

"So then you're saying that it really doesn't matter whether or not we pray," my young friend asks, struggling to understand, "because we're not making God do something God wouldn't do otherwise?"

Only if that were the only way it could matter. Only if prayer's purpose were to change God's mind. But that's not what prayer is for. Prayer doesn't change God. It changes us. It lines us up with the love of God. It points us in the direction of God's love. And when we are pointed in the direction of God's love, we feel its power. We do not bring that power into being—it brought *us* into being. But we line up with it, move with it, allow it to carry us along in its mighty stream.

It carries us, by the way, whether we feel it or not. Praying for your mother when she is near death is different from praying for someone you don't know who is also near death. Your own love, your own fear of losing her, your own complicated history with her, your own grief—they are all there, and you feel them all keenly. Nobody would expect to feel these things about a stranger, and for the purpose of prayer it doesn't matter. Of course you love your mother more than you can possibly love a stranger, but God loves them both the same. That is why your prayer for others does not depend on your feelings for them: prayer joins our love to God's love, and God supplies what we cannot.

The fact that prayer does not hinge on our having the proper feelings does not mean that it is wrong to ask for what we want. God knows of our longing, and we need not pretend a neutrality we do not feel about the outcome of people's situations. By all means, pray for a cure for your cancer, for a new job, for a loving relationship to enter your life. Be honest about that for which you yearn, for God already knows. Your longing is part of you, and the goal in prayer is to bring our whole selves before God.

But whether we pray with specificity for a desired outcome or simply lift our concerns to God without any elaboration, it is important that we not allow the outcome of our situations to become the measure of God's presence in our lives. "There is a God!" people will sometimes say with a laugh when something goes unexpectedly right—a legal parking place appears right in front of their destination. That's a funny line, but it's not really true: there's a God whether we get what we need or not. Life can be very hard: it is full of reverses, and it always ends in death. The presence of God doesn't change that. If prayer were shopping, we'd be able to evaluate God the way we might rate a catalog purchase: Did I get what I ordered? Did it fit? Was it as expected?

But prayer isn't shopping. Millions of the faithful have prayed for the healing of people they loved and then sat and watched them die. The presence of God does not alter the basic facts of human existence, its beginnings, and its endings. Our

· · · · ·

awareness of God's presence is not a means by which we are enabled to manipulate the events of this world by referring them to the power of the next. We simply know that God contains both worlds in a loving embrace. An ancient funeral hymn puts it well:

> You only are immortal,
> The creator and maker of humankind,
> And we are mortal, formed of the dust, and to dust shall we return.
> For so you did you ordain when you created us, saying
> "You are dust, and to dust you shall return."
> All of us go down to the dust;
> Yet even at the grave we make our song:
> Alleluia! Alleluia! Alleluia!
>
> —"Give rest, O Christ," *The Hymnal 1982*, #355

The outcome of my health issues are not the measure of my prayer's efficacy. My prayers' efficacy is measured by the growing certainty within me that I am in God's hands, and that they are always loving hands. In health and illness, in joy and sorrow, in my life and in my death, I am there. I long for cure, but the healing I receive may not be a cure: it may be healing of another kind. Or it may be the complete healing I will find only when I lay my body down for the last time.

· · · · ·

I Join the Club
· · · · ·

I WILL NOT GO to the Club meeting today, even though I feel I should. I will call and plead illness; I *do* have a cold of several weeks' standing, I really *do*. I will surely go next month. Looking back uneasily, I believe I did the same thing last month. My colleagues will think I'm consumptive. That will be fine; it will go nicely with my image as a creative person. We are often unhealthy and attract no untoward attention being so.

But I am not consumptive. I am dispirited.

You can't go to a meeting of your peers visibly dispirited. You have to exude a modest power, a certain satisfaction that tells the assembly that everything in your shop is humming along like a well-oiled machine. You must appear to have no impasse more personally vexing than those arising from the Lutheran-Anglican accord. You need the spiritual energy to deplore current trends in theological education, to rise to your feet and say vehemently that the Church is going to hell in a handbasket, at the same time making it obvious that your own parish is an exception to the downward trend.

So I can't go. My parish *is* going to hell in a handbasket, or so it feels today. Everything seemed to be going so well, I tell my mentors and friends. We've grown a lot. We built this beautiful new chapel. Why are people turning on each other? I arrive early and stay late. Many nights I wrap myself in a sleeping bag and sleep on

· · · · ·

my office floor, not wanting to take the travel time away from my Sisyphean tasks. So weary and full of despair that I can no longer lift my eyes from my desk, I just keep working, running from fire to fire to put them out, writing grant proposals that I should probably find someone else to write and *would*—if I had time to call somebody else. I read about a depressed monkey in a laboratory experiment: kept in a locked room for years, he remained huddled in a corner of it even when the door stood wide open. I am like him. Tears stand in my eyes most of the time when my door is closed, and it is closed more frequently than it has ever been before.

* * *

At night, my eyes fly open in the dark. The house is quiet; not even the footfall of a cat disturbs its stillness. It wasn't my husband's snoring that awakened me—he lies still as a rock, his breathing soft and slow. No, it came from within *me*, this sudden wakefulness, another plague that has descended upon me like an unwelcome in-law. I may be missing some familiar hormones, or perhaps I am adding a few new ones. Whatever. I look at the green numerals on the clock radio. It is two in the morning. *Oh, great,* I think as the work awaiting me at St. Clement's plucks at my sleeve. *Great*—not only must I work myself to death tomorrow, I must also rehearse the whole damn day beforehand, when I'm supposed to be resting up for it.

I run through my repertoire of sleep-inducing tricks. I draw a lovely hot bath and add some aromatherapy potion that my daughter, Anna, says will help me sleep. I bet it cost twenty dollars. I soak in it for a few minutes, and then I begin to breathe deeply, like my yoga teacher told me to: "Soooooo" (inhale) and then "Hummmmm" (exhale). I "So-Hum" for a while, as the lovely smell of the bath surrounds me. I do feel tired. But I still can't sleep

O, all right! I begin the Trisagion: "Holy God, Holy and Mighty, Holy Immortal One, Have mercy upon us." I say it over and over in my mind. The tasks for tomorrow finally settle down, content for now to be carried by the ancient words.

"Why don't I think of prayer earlier in an insomnia attack?" I wonder as the veil of sleep descends at last. God loves me. God knows I need sleep for my busy days, especially now, during these hard ones. So why don't I turn to God sooner? Slow learner, I guess.

* * *

My dreams are of the frustration kind: I'm in a phone booth, and the phone booth is broken. I run for a bus, and I miss it. I'm cooking and can't find the right pot, so I attempt to make soup in a cardboard box on the stove.

* * *

The next day:

I have an enormous writing project I must finish and a grant that must be written and turned in by the end of the day.

Mary is waiting for me at the door.

"Can you give me some money?" she asks in her booming voice. She asks for money every day.

· · · · ·

"How're you doing, Mary?" I remember that I haven't called her social worker to see if there isn't something that can be done about her panhandling. I fumble for my to-do notebook, but I can't find it.

"I married your brother, you know," she says. "I had forty children with your brother."

"Forty's a lot, Mary."

She nods. "Yeah. And I had sixty children in upstate New York before that."

"Gosh. Say, isn't that a new coat? Did you get it from Ann?" I sent her to our thrift shop last time she was in, wearing only a thin sweater against the cold of a December day.

"Yeah."

"You look nice in it. It's a nice warm one."

"Can I have some money?"

* * *

My friend wants to know if I'd like to go with her to the Women's Festival at Madison Square Garden. I didn't know there *was* a women's festival at Madison Square Garden.

Her daughter is in the Vulva Chorus.

"The Vulva Chorus? As in 'vulva'?" I guess I haven't read the paper in a couple of days. But it turns out I can't go; I'll be away.

My daughter will go instead.

. . . . .

"Yeah, I've heard about it," she says.

"It has a Vulva Chorus."

"Yeah, I know. It's about *The Vagina Monologues*, Mom."

"The Vulva Chorus?"

"Yeah. We have to talk about these things now, Mom."

"We do?"

"Yup."

"What do we have to say?"

"That it's great to have one."

"A vagina?"

"Yup. I gotta go."

I *suppose* it's great to have one . . .

* * *

How come there are no penis monologues, my husband wants to know. I tell him I think western literature, by and large, is understood to *be* a penis monologue. He nods, satisfied.

I'm glad both my parents were safely dead before there was such a thing as *The Vagina Monologues*. It's just easier not to get into some things.

* * *

"See if we can hold interruptions for a while," I say to Clarence. "I have to get this

. . . . .

stuff finished." The usual parade of people enters or calls, and I hear him putting them off, which he does by blessing them several times: "Well, now, *thank you* for calling. She's very busy right now, sir, but *thank you* for calling, and if you'll give me your number I'll have her call you when she's free. That's 212? So, thank you, and God bless you no . . . Right, she's just so busy . . . Probably not before three o'clock . . . that's right . . . Well, thank you again for calling and *God bless you,* you hear?"

"You're good, Clarence," I say.

"You got to be," he says. "Ain't no other way."

But a little Muslim lady gets into my office by the back door, though; she must have slipped in the front door with somebody and gone around through the parish hall. She speaks no English, and comes regularly to apologize for that. She points to the sky and says "Allah" and then points at me and bows with her hands folded in front of her. I say "Allah" and bow, too. She reaches into her pocket and brings out one white egg and an aspirin. I exclaim over the gift and say thank you five or six times. She leaves, bowing. Her husband is waiting in the street. They set off down the sidewalk, he with his hands clasped behind his back and she several steps behind.

* * *

The officiant for Evening Prayer hasn't shown up. I forget who it's supposed to be. I climb slowly up the stair to the chapel and put on just enough lights to see. I light the candles. I begin the office. As I often do when I am alone, I chant it. I remember Evening Prayer at seminary. I remember my father. I remember that the words are beautiful. I see the representation of St. Clement's sorrowful face in the stained glass window, and the martyred Jonathan Daniels's next to him. I remember that I am not the only priest in Christendom in a difficult place.

"The Lord be with you," I sing, although there is nobody else in the room. I used to feel foolish doing that, until Brother Justus told me that he never left those greetings out, because the saints and angels are always there with us when we pray. Good point.

"The Lord be with you," I sing.

The saints and angels reply, "And also with you." St. Clement replies, and Jonathan Daniels and Julia Chester Emory from their windows, and Our Lady of Guadeloupe from her shrine, "And also with you." And my mother and father, "And also with you, honey," and my brother, "And also with you." And my friend Denny, who died of AIDS two years ago, "And also with you." "And also with you." All of them, from across the whole stretch of centuries, the saints and angels. Praying with me, loving me, sending me comfort, reminding me that they had trials. Not all of them survived. But all of them still *live*.

Tomorrow is another day. I can turn the grant in first thing. I can find my to-do book and make a list. I can get some sleep. I can admit that my reluctance to go to the Club meeting arises from wounded pride and that I could stand to grow up a bit on that score.

I go back to my office and sit back down at the computer. The candle smells of

· · · · ·

something pungent and vaguely mossy, and the light is soft against the beautiful, dark red walls. The sign on my desk, turned around for others to see, reads "Thank You for Not Whining." I've had it in all my offices for many years. I turn it around so that I might see it, and I start again.

BOTH MEN ARE MEMBERS of the same parish. Both are active. One sits in my office.

Milt's mouth is a grim line as he leans back in my velvet wingchair and crosses his arms. "It's getting so I can't pray at all anymore," he says. "Every time I start, I swear I see Frank's face in my mind, and I get so angry I can't stand it. I mean, I can't pray even when he's nowhere in sight. I even have physical symptoms: my heart pounds so hard I think it's going to jump out of my chest. I can feel the blood pounding in my ears. I think I may have to give up officiating at Evening Prayer. I end up just wanting to put my fist through the wall."

"We've got enough holes in the wall around here already," I tell him. Then I ask him how he prays for Frank, and he looks at me in disbelief. He assumes I have misunderstood.

"Well, I *don't* pray for him. I can't. I just get too mad."

I tell Milt that the first thing that needs to happen is that he needs to be desensitized. "Like those programs for people who are afraid of flying," I say, "where first they take you to a ticket counter, and then they let you practice with an airline seat, and you learn to deal with it, and then you fly, and you're all right."

Right now, just the thought of Frank is enough to send Milt over the edge. First, he needs to cut Frank down to size in his imagination. Frank is taking up valuable real estate in Milt's spirit. Milt can get that space back for something more productive.

· · · · ·

"There is a way to do this," I tell him. "It takes some time, but it will work. Are you game?"

He looks discouraged and shakes his head. But, he wouldn't have brought it up if he didn't want some help with it.

"Well," he says at last, "I sure don't see how. But I really hate being like this. Yeah, so, okay. What do I do?"

"The first thing is that you never, never, *never* pray without praying for Frank."

Milt looks annoyed. He thinks I'm asking him to do the nice Christian thing, where you summon up warm, fuzzy thoughts about people you can't stand. He thinks that making up attractive lies about unattractive feelings is the ticket he must buy in order to gain admission to God's presence. I head him off at the pass.

"Just the name. That's all you have to say. That's all you should do. Just say his name, without an agenda. Just 'Frank.'"

I go on to suggest to him that, when anger is in the driver's seat, we simply cannot be trusted to pray *with* any agenda at all for the one with whom we are angry. If I am deeply angry and begin to pray with an agenda for the one with whom I am angry, it's obvious where I'll end up. I'll end up praying that something on the order of Psalm 35 will happen:

> *Let ruin come upon them unawares;*
> > *let them be caught in the net they hid;*
> > *let them fall into the pit they dug.*
>
> —Psalm 35:8

. . . . .

No, I cannot be trusted to pray *for* anything specific right now. I'm too mad. Instead, just the name is enough.

Milt began to do that: he said Frank's name every time he prayed. Every time.

"How's it going?" I asked one evening after Evening Prayer. Milt had been the officiant. I thought he had seemed a little calmer.

"I'm doing it. That's about all I can say." Milt paused. "At first, it was awful. I'd say his name, and his face would come into my mind, and I wanted to punch his lights out. But now I can say it without going ballistic. So maybe there's been a little progress."

Well, I told him it would take a while . . . and it *did*. But, as time passed, the name of his enemy ceased to be an immovable barrier to Milt's prayer life. It became possible for him to be in the same room as Frank, and then to work on a project of brief duration with him. About six months later, I answered the telephone one evening, and Milt was calling me from Frank's place, where they were having dinner together.

Are they best friends? No. But beginning to pray without agenda for his enemy simply by speaking his name in prayer began the process of removing a grudge from its inappropriate squat in the center of Milt's life and put it on the fringe, where it belonged. Everyone has annoyances, and we all have people we just don't like. But these things shouldn't rule us. The normal negatives of life can run away with us if we allow them to, and then we find ourselves squarely in their grip. Milt had inflated Frank's transgressions until they became all there was to Frank. But nobody is

. . . . .

reducible to his or her sins. Or his or her virtues. We're all more complex than that.

But wait a minute! You can break the back of a terrible anger just by praying the name of the one who has hurt you? After all the bitterness that has passed between you, you're going to get over it by praying his *name*?

Yes. Praying the name without agenda removes us from the management role in this transaction. God knows perfectly well how to deal with Frank. God knows Frank, and God knows Milt, and God created and loves them both. God doesn't need Milt to iron out Frank's behavior or to plan a favorable outcome to their impasse. Milt was too mad to do that anyway. When we present our sorrows to God, God accepts them. The rest is not up to us.

Prayer without agenda works in any arena, not just the arena of anger. "I just don't know what to pray for," someone will say about a mortally ill person; "I don't know if I should pray for her to live or for her to die, she's so terribly ill." As if God might just pull the plug if we pray for the wrong thing. In a very real sense, it doesn't matter what we pray for. What matters is that we pray. Prayer is not an ecclesiastical term for planning—as in those Dear-God-let-Mary-not-have-to-have-her-gall-bladder-out-but-if-she-does-please-make-it-the-kind-that-can-be-removed-laparoscopically-instead-of-the-kind-where-they-cut-you-just-about-in-half prayers into which we sometimes fall. Neither is prayer simply worrying with an "Amen" on the end of it. Prayer joins one's love for someone to God's love for that person. That is all, and it is enough.

For God is free. Praying without agenda for all our concerns puts us in mind of

· · · · ·

God's freedom, helps us to lift our sorrows to the love of God and keep them there. They may break us, these sorrows, but they do not break God. We can trust in God's strength when we are not strong. There is no need for us to enlist God in the service of our desires or our biases: God is free. The love of God in a situation exceeds our love, even our love at its very best.

So don't worry if you don't know what to pray for, and don't let it stop you from starting. All you really have to do is show up.

But doesn't the outcome of my prayer matter? Don't my desires count for anything? If I long for something with all my heart, must I discount that longing, keep it out of God's sight, as if it were a matter of no personal concern to me, as if it were about someone else? Doesn't this "praying without agenda" entail a posture of sanitized relativism that is something less than human?

None of these. It's not the case that our desires don't matter. But prayer is not about seeing to it that our desires prevail. It's about showing ourselves openly to God—grudges, angers, desires, and all—and then allowing God to move in our lives and the lives of those for whom we pray. So, by all means, speak your longing to the God who loves you. But then stay alert. God is free and active in all the changes of life, and frequently—no, always—in ways we do not expect. When Milt began to pray for Frank, he had no expectation and, further, no desire that they would become friends. Plainly, *his* desire was never to set eyes on Frank again. But praying for Frank changed Milt, and it seems to have changed Frank as well.

. . . . .

Besides using the name of a person in prayer without agenda, you can also try picturing him or her in your mind. In the case of an enemy, don't try it too soon: a picture is more vivid than a name and may tap more emotion than you can manage at first. But often, it is ideal: you use your imagination to picture the person—in a very concrete and childish way—lifted up to God. I mean *literally*. Never mind that we all know God isn't really "up" or that we don't really "lift" the things we lift to God. These are images, not facts, so we can be as childish as we wish. In fact, allow me to share with you just how lurid I am in this kind of prayer: when I pray for people in this way, I picture them very small, held on a pair of outstretched hands and lifted high—as garish as the cheapest religious greeting card you could ever buy. Just to make it worse, I also see the picture bathed in golden light. I would not make up such a thing. I have better taste.

You can even use this device when the person for whom you pray is you. Go ahead: picture yourself as a tiny figure nestled in those hands. If you have a hard time doing this, try picturing yourself as you were when you were a child. Remember an outfit you liked to wear and imagine putting it on. Sometimes it's easier to pray for the child than for the compromised adult.

Sure, the images are sentimental. But nobody sees them except me and God, and neither of us is an art critic. Picturing someone in this concrete and sentimental way reminds me that there is a reality larger than that person and her problems, larger than I am, a reality that contains us. It reminds me that we really are all in the hands of God, no matter what. None of us will live forever, and nobody

· · · · ·

gets everything she wants, but none of us is outside the circle of God's love. So I picture us all as very small, held in God's hands, and seeing this image in my mind helps me trust in the reality, whatever my current surroundings. For we *are* all very small. And we *are* all in God's hands.

True Confessions

$\cdot$ $\cdot$ $\cdot$ $\cdot$ $\cdot$

I'M HEARING MORE CONFESSIONS than I used to. Now, why would this be so? Have I become more guilt-inducing with age? If I had, I suppose I'd be the last to know. Maybe it's just a *fin-de-millennium* urge to take stock. Whatever the reason, Confession seems to be on people's radar screens in a way it wasn't a couple of decades ago.

What is the Sacrament of Confession? Technically, it's not called that anymore: it got an image redesign in the seventies—thanks to Prayer Book revision—so now it's called the Sacrament of Reconciliation (more upbeat, in a decade when we had a hard time with the idea that anything might be our fault). You may have grown up in a church that required you to make a sacramental confession before receiving Communion; this was part of any Roman Catholic upbringing. Some people remember this as a shameful and guilty event; others as superficial and glib. At its best, though, confession has nothing to do with shame or with superficial legalisms. It is the act of a spiritual adult who recognizes an action in her past as unworthy of the beloved child of God she knows herself to be, and who desires to be free to do things differently next time.

Primarily, confession is the restoration to community of one who is estranged from it. It is a profound welcome home to one who has spent some time in self-imposed exile. As long as there is something in our history about which we say to

$\cdot$ $\cdot$ $\cdot$ $\cdot$

ourselves, "They wouldn't welcome me if they knew the truth about me," we remain in spiritual isolation. Only when we have allowed God's reconciling love to shine on even the soiled places can we know ourselves to be wholly loved.

Make no mistake: confession has nothing to do with cajoling God into letting us off the hook of our sins. In Christ, God already forgives us everything. Confession and absolution do not "bring about" the divine forgiveness; they merely affirm that which is present, right here, right now. Confession has nothing to do with going to hell or not going there. It is, instead, about opening our hearts to the kind and piercing love of the God who has always known what we have done and why we have done it. Confession doesn't change God's mind. It changes ours.

To whom should you make your confession? Of course, any Christian can confess to any other Christian, including a layperson—it would not be a sacramental confession, but neither would it be a useless exercise. Just be sure that the person to whom you unburden yourself is a person of spiritual maturity who can keep his own counsel (which is why most people who want to confess do so with a priest, who knows very well that the confessional seal is absolute). It may be that this person will not be your own parish priest, but one from another parish; the ancient tradition of anonymous confession, for which confessional booths were used for hundreds of years, has a certain value. Your confession is your only business with such a confessor; you won't be serving on her vestry or voting on his salary. A matter of choice, but one worth considering.

. . . . .

How might you begin to prepare: Your confessor will have some suggestions. Here is what many people who are making a first confession (or the first one in a long, long time) do to prepare:

1. Take several sheets of paper. Begin writing things down—everything you've ever done that you regret. Write whatever comes into your mind. Don't bother with full sentences, correct outline form, chronological order, spelling, or anything else—these are notes, and nobody need see them but you. Don't try to rank your sins; just get them down: anything from using the wrong fork at dinner to capital murder. If you're not sure whether or not something really is a sin, write it down anyway. Your confessor can help you decide later. For now, just spill it. This will take a few evenings. There is no rush.

2. Read through what you've written a few times. Take your time doing so. After two or three readings, you will see that most of what you've written collects around two or three themes: habitual anger, maybe, or over-the-top covetousness. There really aren't many human sins—seven, actually; the same old Seven Deadlies spelled out in medieval times are still pretty much all there is when it comes to sin. Pride, envy, wrath, avarice, sloth, gluttony, lust: I challenge you to come up with one, ancient or modern, that does not fall into one of these categories.

3. Two or three of the Seven Deadly Sins are your personal favorites. We all have them; most of us find ourselves bringing up the same old things every time we make a confession. Slow learners, we are. Bring them to your confession, and talk

. . . . .

them over with your confessor. It is his job to help you discern the difference between things that are sinful and things that are not. You may feel guilty about something that isn't your fault at all. Incest victims, for example, almost always feel ashamed about a sin that really belongs to their abusers, not to them. There's no point in confessing things that aren't sins. Or in confessing other peoples' sins. Most of us have enough of our own to keep us occupied, without borrowing those of others.

4. With your confessor, talk these sins over. Examine them as the lifelong tendencies they are. Talk about concrete ways to change them. Confession involves willingness to change, and to *be* changed. Avail yourself of the confessor's advice, including her knowledge of resources that might help you change.

5. Finally, do the Rite of Reconciliation with your confessor. In the Book of Common Prayer, it is on page 447 (with another, more poetic version immediately following it on page 449). There is a moment within the rite when your confessor offers what the Prayer Book calls "counsel, direction, and comfort." Some of this will reiterate what you explored in your talk before the rite. The confessor may suggest something for you to add to your spiritual routine for a while: a psalm on which to meditate; a scripture passage to ponder daily for a week or two; a book you might read to consider a particular issue in more depth. These suggestions are what traditionally has been called a "penance," the subject of so many "Say ten Hail Marys and call me in the morning" jokes. I prefer that a penance be edifying, rather than simply a chore: related to the issues arising

· · · · ·

from the confession, and likely to assist you in changing the behavior that troubled you enough to send you to confession in the first place.

6. Confession ends in absolution. The priest pronounces God's forgiveness of your sins and makes the sign of the cross on your forehead. Many people, especially those who have been dreading this moment for years, are surprised by a remarkable feeling of freedom. If you've been carrying a couple of heavy valises full of sins you've never talked with anyone about, it feels darn good to set them down. You may find that you feel oddly tired; if that is so, go home and take it easy, with a nice bath and a cozy bed. Making a confession is hard work. You probably need a rest.

* * *

This may have been your first confession, but it need not be your last. You can avail yourself of this rite any time. The pithy Anglican saying "All may, none must, some should" sums up our attitude toward it exactly: it is another gift God gives us through the Church, and it is ours to use for our good. Over a period of years, you will know the resignation of chalking up the same sorts of sins over and over again, familiar enemies of your well-being. You will tell your confessor something like, "It's the usual suspects this time. *Again.*" and you will both shake your heads. But it is a very good thing in life, and a rare one in this world of ours, to have a person to whom you can say that, and know that she will understand exactly what you mean.

. . . . .

MRS. WILLIAMS AND MRS. RALSTON were the *grandes dames* of my childhood church. Everything about them told you so. Their attire was much richer than everybody else's. Mrs. Williams wore beautiful suits in jewel colors, fantastic hats made of feathers and flowers, and pristine, long white gloves with beautiful shirring and tiny pearl buttons up the side of them. She wore a fur, also: the kind to which the minks' heads were still attached. We children were fascinated by it: the tiny feet, the tail, the little glaring, amber eyes.

Mrs. Ralston also had a mink, though it was of much less zoological interest: a simple stole worn around the shoulders of *her* exquisite suits, every bit as beautifully made and brightly colored as Mrs. Williams's. As a rule, Mrs. Ralston's hats were higher than Mrs. Williams's, who favored wider brims to balance her taller figure.

Mrs. Ralston sat near the front on what was known in those days as the "epistle side," the right side of the nave as one faced the altar. Mrs. Williams sat in the back row of that side, and was the first of any of us to arrive, since her husband, Stuart, as small and meek and resigned a man as his wife was large and formidable, was the usher and needed to be at his station early to pass out the service leaflets. There they would be when worshipers walked in, Mrs. Williams greeting each arrival like a queen and Stuart fussing over his pile of leaflets. She greeted them all, that is, except

· · · · ·

one: when Mrs. Ralston made her own queenly entrance, not a word was exchanged, not a word or a glance.

* * *

It has been so for decades. I used to pester my mother and grandmother about why the two ladies didn't speak, but they answered vaguely, and I knew it was a secret. At the church suppers—turkey in the fall and fried chicken in the spring—Mrs. Williams ruled the kitchen with martial authority, her merest glance securing compliance even from immense men brandishing potato mashers. Her steaming plates poured forth from the kitchen; the exquisite smell summoned the countryside for acres around the church.

Mrs. Ralston ruled the dining room. That is where we girls worked: serving the diners, taking pie orders from among the breathtaking array on the pie table—peach, apple, pumpkin, coconut custard, blueberry, lemon meringue, chocolate, butterscotch, pecan, banana cream. And we would trot to the biscuit table, where Mrs. Thompson mixed feathery biscuits and baked them in a small covered oven right on the spot, so they were steaming and fresh when we laid them in baskets on the tables. And we would fetch glasses of sweet iced tea, sweet being the only kind they made. The older ladies would stand beside empty seats and hold up two and three and four fingers to signify the presence of vacancies, and Mrs. Ralston reigned over it all.

It was an economy that could only have worked in a tiny country church like that one, I suppose: two parish leaders who never communicated with each other. It had been like this for so long that everyone had long since learned how to manage the little cold war, and nobody gave it much thought.

Nobody but the rector. He was new to the parish, his first cure, and full of a true goodness that would last the entire forty years he served that little church and a smaller one ten miles north. It was a terrible thing to him that these two ladies should have carried on a grudge for all those years, and a terrible thing that the church had let them. He made inquiries as to the origins of the estrangement, and got nowhere: small towns do not yield up their secrets quickly. This, too, was annoying. But there was one more thing he could try.

He knew from his study of the Prayer Book that there was a provision in it allowing the minister to refuse communion to those in his parish

> betwixt whom he perceiveth malice and hatred to reign; not suf-
> fering them to be partakers of the Lord's Table, until he know them
> to be reconciled.
>
> —General Rubrics for Holy Communion
> The Book of Common Prayer, 1928, p. 85

And so he spoke to each of the ladies privately. They would not be admitted to Communion the next Sunday unless they spoke to each other.

* * *

Everyone was in church the following week. Even my mother and grandmother (who usually arrived just in the knick of time) got there early, and they had told me that I must always be above gossip in the parish. Mrs. Williams, of course, was already seated. One of the minks caught my eye with a malicious amber gleam, and I quickly looked away. Stuart fretted over his leaflets with more than the usual melancholy.

Enter Mrs. Ralston. Her process down the aisle was as always, stopping here and there to accept somebody's hand. And then she turned and spoke.

"Good morning, Mrs. Williams."

"Good morning, Mrs. Ralston."

And then she sat down in her pew. The rector, half hidden in the sacristy doorway, heard the exchange. And the silence after it. He thought a moment and then signaled the organist to begin the processional.

It was not all he had hoped. Still, they had spoken.

* * *

It was not until twenty years later that my mother finally told me why Mrs. Williams and Mrs. Ralston never spoke. They had grown up together in that little town, two girls about the same age. They had gone to the same school and the same church. In her teens, Mrs. Ralston had become pregnant out of wedlock. In a plan that may seem strange and even cruel to us now but was not uncommon then, she and her mother remained at home in seclusion until the baby was born, whereupon her mother presented the child to the world as her own and they resumed their lives as if nothing had happened. The little girl reached adulthood never knowing that the woman she thought to be her sister was really her mother. These facts were known by almost everyone. But by silent common consent, they were never discussed.

Somewhere along the line, though, Mrs. Williams had made a snide remark to someone about Mrs. Ralston's secret, and Mrs. Ralston had heard about it. I think of the shame of the young girl in her embarrassing situation, of her strange loss of what the world considers honor, of her daily proximity to her child without a mother's place in that child's history. Even after she married Mr. Ralston, she never had another child. How cruel a thing it must have been to hear that a friend had gossiped maliciously about her. I believe that, except for the exchange in the church aisle that Sunday morning, they never spoke again in this life.

That's a long time to carry a grudge.

But here it is: I have to forgive others if I wish, myself, to feel forgiven and free. Those two ladies in the little old church lived long and productive lives, and were good to many people. Those turkey dinners! Those chicken dinners! But there was a piece missing out of each of them that cannot have done either of them any good. They could not find a way to forgive. More than anything else, this fact stops people cold in the project of finding reconciliation, with God and with other human beings. It sounds to them as if they are being asked to do something they know they cannot do: somehow come up with a great rush of warm, friendly feelings toward someone who has hurt them terribly. It sounds as if any forgiveness God might have for them will be hostage to the improbable completion of this task; as if the one who has hurt them must somehow be allowed to get away with it—his crime erased and forgotten; as if they must somehow learn to adopt an oh-what-the-heck-that's-okay attitude toward people who have injured them grievously. But that's not what forgiveness is.

Sins aren't okay. By definition, they're not okay; if they were okay; they wouldn't be sins, would they? There would be no need for forgiveness. What we would be talking about if sins were okay would be acquittal, not forgiveness. Acquittal means the guy didn't do it. He walks. He's innocent. But when we forgive, that's not the judgment we're making. We're not exonerating. We're just electing to move on. Forgiveness turns out to be much more about you than about the one who has hurt you.

In a curious way—curious and offensive to many people, I might add—the distinction between the victim of a wrong and its perpetrator is not as central to the problem of forgiveness as it always seems. This thought runs so counter to the way almost all of us feel that it sounds like nonsense, especially to the victim of a grave injury.

Wait a minute! . . . you're saying that there's no difference between me and the one who betrayed my trust so completely that I don't think I can ever trust again?

Whether I committed the sin or someone else committed it against me is not as important to my eventual freedom as is ejecting it from its inappropriate place in the spotlight on my spiritual landscape. Whoever did it—if it is obsessing me—I am the one who must act to change things. As fascinated as we cannot help but be with

· · · · ·

the question "Who started it?" the more urgent and more useful question is "Who can end it?" The first is a question about the past, and we cannot change the past. But the second is about the present and the future, and these are things we can affect by our own agency.

Please don't be so disgusted by the last paragraph that you stop reading. I have not said there is no such thing as right or wrong. Of course there is. Certainly there are such things as aggression, as dishonesty, as faithlessness. There are also degrees of injury: failing to RSVP and burglary are not of equal gravity. From the viewpoint of my soul's health, though, my inability to move on from a wrong that has been done me may be much more troublesome, over a much longer stretch of time, than the original wrong ever was. Whether I did it or had it done to me, I am the only one who can offer it to God to be removed from its hurtful place in my heart. In that sense, and in that sense alone, sins against me can function in my heart as if they were my own.

You have known someone, I'm sure, who nourished a grudge for decades. Perhaps you have even *been* someone who nourished a grudge for decades—in utter estrangement from someone with whom you once were close. Often, it is a former spouse who occupies that Siberia. I've known many divorced people who, ten or fifteen years after the breakup, describe it at almost every social gathering with as fresh a hurt and anger as if it had happened the previous week. Over and over they review their own innocence and the perfidy of the former husband or wife for anyone who will still listen. Their tragedy has become liturgical: it has chronology and

. . . . .

cause—credal and immutable—that must not be altered. It has only one allowable meaning.

And who knows? Maybe she is right, the wounded innocent. The fault may be completely and utterly his, and she may have been totally without blame in the breakup of their marriage. This would be rare, but it is conceivable. She may be innocent. But she is far from free. She is probably much more imprisoned by the sin of her ex than he has ever been. He may have sinned grievously against her twenty years ago, but it is she who carries the heavy baggage of his sin with her still, she who still nurses the ongoing bitterness of an ancient betrayal. It's hard work, carrying someone else's load like that.

How can she ever get free?

I'm pretty sure she won't get free by putting forth an enormous effort of will to forgive. If this could have been done through an exercise of her will, it probably *would* have been. Her will is crippled, at present, by many things—her anger, her hurt, her embarrassment.

We might as well be honest here and admit that forgiveness does not come naturally to us. We are not forgiving by nature. We are vengeful. We tend to hang onto things, not let go of them. By ourselves, we are not good at this.

But we are not by ourselves.

The life of faith is not about becoming a better and better person through a superhuman effort of will. It is about connecting with the power of a loving God. Is forgiveness beyond you? Of course it is: it's beyond all of us. But it is not

· · · · ·

beyond the one who looked down upon his tormentors from the cross and understood them. And because that one lives in us, we can lay hold of this loving power and move beyond terrible things, if we must. With the power that comes from our loving creator through a loving redeemer, we can do things we otherwise could not do.

We begin to forgive by deciding, not by feeling. It is a theological decision, not one guided by the human limitations we must ordinarily take into consideration when we decide about many other things, like which school to attend or which car to buy. We make the decision to forgive knowing that we lack the power to carry it out, and so we make it asking for that power to be given to us as God wills. Our feelings don't lead us to forgiveness; they usually lead us in the opposite direction. We begin by deciding to allow God to enter into our process of dealing with our feelings and their continuing grip on us. God understands our feelings and their great power over us very well. God knows us. In making this beginning, we have nothing to fear: God is gentle with us and knows full well that our feelings of terrible anger mark the moment in our history when something terrible happened to us. God is not in the business of explaining it all away or insisting that we do that. God does not brainwash us or demand that we brainwash ourselves.

Part of deciding to forgive may involve bringing your inability to do so to confession. How might you do this? The Office of Compline on page 127 of The Book of Common Prayer contains one prayer of confession; it's the only one of the Daily Offices in which the confession is not optional, on the sensible theory that the end of the day is a good time to take inventory, and that, in doing so, most of us will be able to unearth at least one thing in the course of the day just past that we wish we hadn't done. So maybe you could start there, for a night or two, and see what happens.

Or maybe this is a matter better suited to a sacramental confession. Maybe you need the accountability of having another person in the room to help you make yourself accountable to God. This can be a frightening prospect: I'm supposed to expose this to another human being? What if he gives me a lecture about turning the other cheek and sends me on my way with a pat on the head? What if he thinks I'm selfish and mean-spirited? What if he tells me I have no right to feel as I do?

Well, for heaven's sake, choose your confessor with care. Don't go to someone you already know to be a grown-up hall monitor, or to someone who routinely ignores other people's feelings and concerns. Go to someone with whom you have a good rapport and whose probity is beyond question.

Your confession of being unable to forgive is only that: it is not a reopening of the case against the one who has injured you to determine, yet again, his guilt or innocence. It is only an honest admission that your experience of that hurt has taken over more of your life than is healthy. It is not nearly as much about the original injury as it is about how your life has been since then. It is not so much about a stubborn refusal to forgive as about a lamentable inability to do so, an inability even to *begin*. It's not so much about your willful "I won't!" as it is about your sorrowful "I can't; can you help me?" There are rocks we can't lift. There are lots of

· · · · ·

them. We shouldn't try to lift them ourselves. We should ask for the help we need. Confessing our weakness opens us to this help.

When we ask God for help in our weakness, we get help. Ordinarily it is not immediate, a melting away of decades of hostility in an instant. Often—usually—it doesn't look much like our expectation or our plan. But in the act of asking, we have received.

Now it can begin to make sense to talk about a "theological decision" to forgive. Now we remember that our feelings *often* lag behind our decisions. Now we understand that the decision to forgive is not certified by the sudden blossoming of good feelings. The theological decision to forgive does not need certification as real; if you have said it to God, it has already begun to happen. In deciding to forgive, in some sense, you have done so. And this is true even if you're just as mad as you ever were. You may still be mad, but you are not alone. You have asked God into the mix of your feelings and your decision, and now you have a power much greater than your own at work in you, sorting things out. Right here, right now, the process of easing your burden has begun.

So "forgive and forget" is nothing but an alliterative illusion. Forgiveness does not erase history or exonerate. History has happened, and nobody can revise its content or many of its consequences. And feelings are not the barometer of forgiveness in its early stages, although with the passage of time they heal powerfully in a person who has turned to God for help in living a forgiving and forgiven life.

. . . . .

Poor Mrs. Williams. Poor Mrs. Ralston. Gone to their graves years ago, now, those frozen dead places still locked in their hearts. No doubt they are friends again. But it could have happened while they still lived here. The dead places could have filled with light and life and love in this life.

FOR THE MOST PART, religious speech doesn't make much sense. That fact is a powerful obstacle squarely in the path of modern people. We are people who want to be clear. We want words to mean exactly what they say, and no more. We don't want there to be shades of meaning. We want our spiritual speech clear and unambiguous, too. We want it to make sense, the way other kinds of speech—recipes, directions, news bulletins—make sense.

But "sense," of course, is about the phenomenal world. "Sense" is about matter, about space and time, about the laws of physics. And the things of the spirit are not confined to the categories of the phenomenal world. If the things of the spirit could make perfect sense, they wouldn't be the things of the spirit. They would, instead, be descriptions of the way things are on earth—valuable and interesting to many of us, no doubt, but not occupying any space beyond that which we can readily approach by the familiar means we employ when we want to know something about our world: How big is it? When did it happen? What color is it? Does it work? What is it for?

The things of the spirit are not about our world. They show themselves here, but they refer to a larger reality, the reality that contains this one. Some of the most important categories of our world—the category of time, for example—are irrelevant to the larger spiritual reality. Time is our great organizer, the means by which

· · · · ·

we measure and view our lives. Time is our great enemy: it ushers us, inexorably and without exception, toward the grave. Not one of us escapes.

But, in the dominion of God, time does not exist. We cannot imagine this. We think of time as a line, and it measures everything for us: Before the war. After my son died. The year I finished school. While I was living in Duluth. After I came home from France. We try to do that with God's dominion, too: we simply place it at the end of our line. We call it the "Afterlife." But we probably need a new name for it. It isn't the last stop on the train of time. It isn't just "after" this life; it's all around it.

What can the timelessness of God mean for us, whose lives are utterly determined by the passage of time? Let's consider a couple of possibilities.

Sigmund Freud, in describing the layers of human memory and their power in the human psyche, used this image: imagine an archeological dig, like the many-layered excavation of the city of Troy that fascinated the world when Freud was young. For generations, people had assumed that the city was a myth, that it had no existence in antiquity save in the great epic poem we know as *The Iliad*. But it was not so: Troy was discovered beneath the gravel on its traditional site. It turned out there really was a Troy. The excavation took years, and eventually revealed not one but seven cities, one beneath another. There had been many Troys. Each had supplanted its predecessor in the same place as time moved on. If a visitor were to look at a cross section of the dig, a vertical slice, the levels would have been plainly distinguishable: the dusty plain of the site, abandoned in modern times, the medieval city, the city of the classical world, the Bronze Age city, the Neolithic village, the rudimentary camp of the first hunter-gatherers to put down stakes in that place. There it would be, a visual journey through the centuries in a certain place, dead city layered upon dead city, each city silently holding its forgotten secrets.

The human psyche is like that, Freud said, with one marvelous difference: all the cities are still alive.

Imagine a cross section of the archeological dig now, each level full of activity, of meals cooking and children crying, of deals being struck and rituals observed, all alive, all at once, not a single level still and silent. That's what your mind is like, Freud said: everything that has happened to you is still alive in you. Your infantile trauma is not over; it is still being enacted in your behavior as an adult.

A century of exposure to Freud and his legatees has acquainted most of us with this idea. Many of us know that events of long ago freshly inform our ways of being in the world today. That human psychology should work this way is no longer news.

But I think the kingdom of God works this way, too. The linear, before-and-after progression of history as we know it does not exist in that reality. Everything in the dominion of God is *now*. It's all present. It's not "after"; it's "also."

I stand beside a hospital bed and weep to see my mother shudder a final breath and then stop. Stop forever, I think, with a finality that breaks my heart. Never to be seen again. Never. Never. Those anguished words sit in our hearts like lead, and we think that we simply cannot bear it. The decades in which we will walk the earth unaccompanied by that dear presence stretch brutally out before us, a cruel highway on which we must travel alone.

But *their* path is a different one. They awaken immediately to a wider life, a blinding light that gives paradoxical clarity, a way of being that unites the whole chain of their earthly history in one eternal moment. They step out of our tragedy, the one they shared with us, pick it up, tuck it under one arm and start off down a new road. But the new road is not the afterlife; it is the *also*life. Because we are still with them. The endings that hurt us so are not endings to them. They have no time anymore, for they are out of our world of time and space. And so nothing is lost to them.

They are outside of time, and so nothing is lost.

If this idea seems bizarre and a bit slippery, I ask you to reserve judgment for now. It has taken decades for these things to dawn on me, and that is just what they have done: dawned. They have dawned, slowly, and they are still dawning. It has not been the case that I just got it with a sudden click. Perhaps others get it like that, but not I. Slow learner.

You probably know that some of the stars we see at night are no longer there. It seems that the distances in space are so enormous that light, as fast as it travels, takes billions and billions and probably trillions and God knows how many other kinds of -illions of years to reach the retina of my eye so that I may see those stars. In the eons that have intervened between the glowing moment of the stars I now behold and the present time, something untoward doubtless has happened to some of them.

. . . . .

They have blown up, or burned out, done whatever it is that stars do when it's all over for them. But that news hasn't traveled to my eye yet. I'm still seeing an earlier moment, a moment long past.

It is not stars I'm seeing: it is their ancient light. It is light that has traveled long and far to meet my gaze. Light is a form of energy. We reflect that energy: people can see each other because light reflects from them and hits the retinas of those who see them.

Now let us imagine that there were very sensitive, fine telescopes and instruments, capable of discerning even the feeble flickers of energy we reflect, from a great distance. Suppose that someone far away trained those fine instruments on us. There we would be, caught in the cross hairs of their superior telescopy. But it wouldn't be us *now*, would it? By the time they saw us, so far away, we would be long gone, dead, burned out, like the ancient stars I see at night that exist no longer. So somewhere, for someone, sometime, I can be seen at age five. Someone can see me middle-aged—as I am now—at a time when I have been dead for millennia. Lost to this world, I'll be plainly seen in that one. And my mother, and my father, and my brother. And yours. Everyone and everything, still seen. Still.

Just a metaphor. Maybe it will help. I, for one, like the idea of someone watching me and my mom argue thirty years ago about whether I wore too much make-up.

God must see things this way: everything, all at once. An image—vivid if somewhat disrespectful—comes to mind: God with a compound eye like insects have, all the little facets filled with the complex vision of everything that is. Of course we don't know if God has eyes like a housefly. Probably not. But we do begin to understand that God is really different from us—and sees differently; and that making sense in human terms is so far south of the divine nature that there's little point in bringing it up.

God is spirit, and spirit is not about space and time. Pondering the domain of God in this, beginning with its timelessness, is slippery and paradoxical. (No wonder nobody has ever understood the Incarnation of Jesus Christ, where the two domains meet!) God's timelessness can even be offensive to us, because of what it entails about the judgment of God: as we consider the alsolife, it soon begins to occur to us that the sorting mechanisms of which we are so fond may not be as permanent as we have always thought they were. If, in the eternal present of God, all that has ever been still is, and the same is true for all that will be, if the linearity of our world dissolves in the wholeness of God's experience, then the events of this life may not be as determinative as we think they are. We are bound by history here on the earth, but that is only so here. God is not bound by history. God is free. Our tradition acclaims God as lord of history; God is shown in history but stands outside it—or, rather, contains it. All of history happens within the alsolife—all the past, all the present, all the future, simultaneously present in God's eternal Now.

Including some uncomfortable things. The moment of resurrection is there, but so is the moment of death. My healing is there, but so is my illness. "Doesn't sound

. . . . .

72

like much of a heaven to me," a man in one of my classes snorts. But think: these things are no longer separated from one another by time. There *is* no time. Our misery does not go on and on, year after year, in the larger life, as it did on earth. It collapses into a single timeless image of existence, as does all our other experience. And the divine love that created us here is the same love that lives there, the same love in which, St. Paul tells us, "Christ will be all in all." God lives a life that triumphs over death, an existence that triumphs over non-existence.

The ancient Christians considered evil to be "a privation of the good." By that they meant that evil was fundamentally non-existence: the destruction of life, of joy, the ruin of love, the perversion of right. Every evil could be stated in terms of a subtraction from a more fundamental good. But in the alsolife, in which all is seamlessly in Christ, no subtraction, no diminution occurs. God is the "maker of all that is, seen and unseen." *Is-ness* is what God is, not *is-not-ness.*

Spinning the times and events of our lives out into a limitlessness that confounds them, thinking of evil as something which, in a profound way, literally does not exist in the larger life—these things are hard to hold in one's mind. They are a considerable distance from the simple economy most of us have carried with us as a religious inheritance: this life is a test, graded either with fiery failure in hell or an endless church service in heaven. The great Christian epic about this, of course, is Dante's *The Divine Comedy,* of which by far the most interesting part is *Inferno,* with its detailed descriptions of the ongoing suffering of the damned. We read this 800-year-old poem, though, and notice that many of the damned are people whose names we do not recognize, parties to this or that very local fracas in thirteenth-century Florence, in which Dante wrote. We see that heaven and hell have been domesticated, then and now, to be a means of social control within the human community. We visit the cathedrals of Europe and gaze upon frescoes, stone carvings, stained glass windows depicting of the Last Judgment, and we see that the damned are always much more interesting in their novel tortures than the homogenous good in their white robes. Whatever you do—these depictions instruct us—don't be one of the damned: disembowelment by devils; hideous forms of rape by devils; you-name-it done by devils to miserable sinners as the eternal and terrible wages of their deeds on earth.

We grow up to take all this with a certain circumspection: we can easily see that much of Christian teaching about the afterlife is culturally conditioned and that some of it is politically motivated. Wishing not to be superstitious or gullible, we nonetheless sense a missing *something* in liberal religious thought, which has but a small will to engage any existence save the one we are living now. We know ourselves to be limited in our understanding. We draw back from the optimistic faith in human reason that has so conditioned our faith since the Enlightenment. Even our science has taught us of things we cannot see, and we believe in them. But still, a cosmos about which we understand more than ever before is somehow more mysterious than ever.

At the very least, this new humility about our own vision should give us new courage to contemplate, with open heart and mind, the vision and ways of God in creation, never assuming God to be limited as we are limited, never assuming that only things we can comprehend can be true. Human reason is a human tool. It exists as a gift from God so that we can live in our world and manage what we find here. But we have always known that it falls short of the wisdom of God. So we use it here, through a glass darkly, but should not expect to rely on it exclusively in an existence that transcends it, where we will know as we are known.

A Present From My Grandfather
. . . . .

I NEVER KNEW MY GRANDFATHER. He died before I was born. He brought his family to this country from the north of England in the twenties: my grandmother, my father, and his three brothers. They came first to Saskatchewan and then to North Dakota, where my grandfather served several tiny churches.

O, the Dakotas were bleak! A person could travel a long way without seeing a single tree. In those days the bleached skulls of cattle still lay by the side of the road where the poor things had fallen in their exhaustion or hunger. Balls of tumbleweed hurtled along the prairie for miles and miles, their progress uninterrupted by accident of vegetation or topography. The habitations, too, were bleak, their paint whipped thin, the wood laid bare by the wind.

In a photograph of the church's interior, my grandparents stand in the sanctuary, she at the lectern and he in the pulpit. She wears a baggy thirties dress, but her hair is just as it was when I came along decades later: braided and wrapped in a coronet around her head, innocent of the marcelled fashion of the day. He is more timeless: he could be any clergyman anywhere, any time in the twentieth century. It must be Thanksgiving: the church is decorated with leaves and pumpkins and produce. The pulpit in which he stands has become an immense bundle of cornstalks, and a heap of fruits and vegetables almost conceals the altar. A garland of leaves begins at the pulpit, peaks at a point over the crossing and

. . . . .

descends to the lectern. Both of them are smiling with pride. "This is lovely," they said to the ladies who decorated the church. "Just lovely. You've done a splendid job!"

I look at the picture again. Now their smiles look a little brave. Truth to tell, the place looks awful. It looks like somebody overturned a fruit stand in there. Still they smiled. I think they must have been very kind.

In another picture, they stand in the yard before their faded frame house. My great-grandmother has come to live with them now from England. They all squint into the camera. A hard life in a hard place. I also have pictures of the place they left behind: a big, comfortable, stone house, a large Edwardian family, all the little girls in white dresses, all the boys in high collars. Many aunts, many uncles. I can see from the pictures that my vocation, which feels so unique and personal to me, would be seen by them as nothing more than my having gone into the family business: half the men in the group wear preaching tabs. My entry into it would have surprised them only because of my gender.

I have their account book from those years on the prairie, a long, narrow, leather one. The stipend he took from his cure was pitiably small, and I see that there were years in which it was not paid in full, months in which milk or eggs or a delivery of coal, the tithes of the cash-poor, were substituted for money. I see that my grandmother gave piano lessons and that lessons yielded a quarter apiece. I see that my grandfather traveled from church to church in a wagon, drawn by a horse that I remember my father saying was called Daisy Perkins; in the account book, I see that

Daisy Perkins, too, was sometimes the recipient of parishioners' largesse, in the form of hay and oats.

I do not know for sure why they came here. Why they left comfort and familiarity for a new, hard place. It cannot have been easy, not the trip and certainly not the life they found. But they never again returned to their home across the sea. My father just said they came because they were called.

My grandfather collapsed on a railroad platform on his way home from a church meeting. He remained conscious long enough to be taken home and for my father to get there. As my father watched, counting the seconds between each breath, my grandfather lay comatose. Suddenly he sat up and looked at something in the distance no one else could see. His blue eyes were "blazing," my father said as he told me this story, and I am as faithful to their "blazing" when I tell it now as a child is to the order in which the three bears deal with their porridge. "I always knew you would come for me," said my grandfather, looking into another world, and then he lay back down and died.

I always knew you would come for me.

That is the only present I have from him, and it is enough. To leave a little girl this story, the story of a grandfather whose faithful life had taught him to expect his savior to come and help him into the next world, and who was not disappointed. Whose trust in the God he had served for so long, and with such devotion, was stronger than his fear of dying. Who had so little but, in the end, wanted for nothing.

· · · · ·

We can't do much to change the day of our death or the manner of our dying. But we can give a gift to those who must watch us leave and whose lives will be changed by our leaving: the gift of seeing us embrace the end of this life and the beginning of the new one with confidence. We can leave them a legacy of trust instead of a legacy of fear. We can show them this, and they can carry it with them for the rest of their lives, and then they can give it to the ones who will stand around them as they take their leave.

It was not just a gift for me. It was a gift for my father, too. And my father remembered it, and he passed it along.

And then he gave me another one.

My parents used to read Compline together. I could hear them from my room, his rich, deep "The Lord be with you" and my mother's lighter "And also with you." It was night music, sweet night music to which to fall asleep. Always the same, a "good-night" that never varied, a ritual the very syllables of which still make me feel ready for sleep, no matter what has transpired during the day.

Her death was not unexpected. Not by me, at any rate. She was always frail, a frailness that became increasingly profound in the several years before her death. My father, though, seemed to have found a way not to know that she was dying. He had always thought he would die first, a belief shared by most men. That would have been my choice, had I been doing the planning: my mother was more prepared to be a widow than he to be a widower, I thought. But my advice was not sought. On the day she died, we left her there in the hospital, went to the funeral home to do the funeral things, stopped at the grocery store for something or other, and trifled with some toast and tea at home before giving up and going to bed.

Full of my own sorrow and his, I undressed in my old room, in my old bed, which had been my mother's when she was little, and her mother's when she was little. My father was august: tall, in those days, with a soldierly stride and erect carriage. His voice was deep, rich: people who knew him still tell me how lovely it was to hear him read the gospel. He was wise, consulted by everyone about everything, for his wisdom was almost a visible thing, like something the eye could detect. I don't think most people knew how dependent he was upon my mother, not as much for care and cooking as for emotional anchoring. How on earth was he going to manage without her? I slid into bed and pulled the covers up to my chin. The familiar feel of the little bed and the softness of the old sheets were more than enough to bring the tears, and I lay alone with them for several minutes. Presently, though, I heard a muttering from their room—my father's room, now, I supposed, unpleasantly jarred by the thought that he suddenly had a room of his own. The muttering was his, and he was saying Compline all by himself.

And I knew that he would be all right. Although this was, without question, the worst thing that had ever happened to him, he would find his way through it. He had the treasure of this ancient rhythm, long established in his life, on which to lean. He had a peg upon which to hang his broken heart, a well-trodden path to the God whose strength and comfort he would need. He knew where to turn when his world turned upside down.

. . . . .

Please do not wait until your world turns upside down to begin forming a spiritual discipline that can carry you like that. Do it now. When tragedy lays us low, we're in no shape to set about erecting a spiritual discipline. We can barely tie our shoes. Begin now, while you're in relatively good shape, so that, when you are in desperate need of a way to pray, you won't have to create one out of whole cloth.

Start now. Start by trying on the things of the spirit to see which of them fit you best. Or think of it like painting a boat; lay down layer after tough layer of spiritual practice and prayer, tough layers like coats of paint, so that you have something strong and tough to keep out the rising water in your time of great need. It is certainly not true that God won't come to your help if you haven't done your homework: God comes to you all the time, no matter what. It is your coming to God that slips through the cracks when you have been dealt a body blow. But if you walk a holy path now, day by day, it will be ready for you when you are not sure you can walk at all.

YOU ARE MY GRANDDAUGHTER. You are eleven years old. It is not my expectation that you will read this until you are older. I don't know if you've read my other books—pieces of them, I guess, the parts that are about you. I can't think you'd seek out this little essay—at least, not yet.

But you might when you're older. Specifically, you might when I have died, and you and your sister and your mommy and your aunt are going through my things. After *my* parents died I wanted to read everything they left lying around. I hungered for their presence between the lines. I saved letters, old sermons, recipes, even checkbook registers for a while. We consume the words of the beloved dead in great thirsty gulps, hoping somehow to find again the feeling of them alive. And sometimes we do find a lick of it here and there: a snatch of presence, the sudden scent of a long-ago perfume, a few bars of a forgotten song. We go looking for these things among their written words, and we usually find a few scraps.

What I'm leaving lying around here is important. I want you to know some things about what life in America was like when I was little, long before even your mother was born. If I sat you down and told you, you'd be embarrassed, and I don't want to embarrass you. But I do want you to know.

When I was four, I embarrassed my mother by proclaiming to our maid, "Marjorie, you're chocolate, and we're vanilla."

When I was five, I found my mother crying in front of the television set. I had never seen her cry. She was watching the news: a little girl walking to school, carrying a book bag like the one I carried to school. The street along which she walked was lined with adults: they were coming at her from the crowded sidewalk, coming too close, shouting at her, putting their twisted faces too close to her face and shouting at her. "What are they doing?" I asked. My mother turned off the television and went upstairs.

When I was little, we had drinking fountains labeled "Whites Only" and "Colored." We had separate restrooms and separate motels—called "Colored Cabins." A place out on Route 1 kept that sign up until well into the seventies. You never saw a black person eating in a restaurant where white people ate. I don't think I ever saw one shopping for clothing where I shopped.

One day on the television, I saw the Governor of Alabama standing in the door of a school. He wouldn't let black students into the school. There were soldiers all around him. Another day, I saw three or four young people sitting at a soda fountain waiting to be served. A large white man stood behind the counter, staring at them, paralyzed, not knowing what to do.

In the third grade, our teacher had something important to tell us on the last day of school. "Colored children are going to come here to school next year," she said. "They have to. We have to let them." Her face was without expression. But no colored children came in fourth grade. Or in fifth. Neither did they come the next year. And then I went to school in the next town, to junior high school. Ella Lou was in my seventh-grade class. She was smart and dark and guarded. Another girl put her hand on Ella's arm once. "Quit it!" Ella said quickly and jerked her arm away. On her notebook, where most of us used to write boys' names and the names of favorite records, Ella wrote the name of her old school.

Yardley, the company that made my grandmother's lavender cologne, also had a fragrance called "Bond Street." In town, the colored people's neighborhood ran along Bond Street. Kids used to see that cologne in the drug store. "Oh, why don't you get some Bond Street?" they'd say archly, and everybody would laugh.

Nancy O'Hara dated a black basketball player in ninth grade; he was a senior. Frances Davis dated a black boy. They were the only two. Nancy's parents sent her to boarding school the next year. Frances stayed, and didn't date anybody after that. After high school, Steve Morris dated a black girl whose name I don't recall. I do remember that she was smart. He had been president of the student council.

One summer, a village of tents sprang up on the Mall in Washington, D.C. It was called Resurrection City. It was a tent city of black people, spending weeks in the capital in protest against racism. I went there to talk to them; I thought I might write an article for the local newspaper. I sat on the ground beside a young woman. Could I ask her some questions? "Should I talk to her?" she asked a young man nearby. He looked at me indifferently and shrugged. I felt foolish. I stammered out a few silly questions—"What is Watts like?"—and received monosyllabic replies. I never wrote the story.

Martin Luther King had been shot during the night. I found out about it when

· · · · ·

I woke up. On television, people were burning buildings and getting shot. A man walked by, carrying an enormous television set. Dr. King's coffin traveled along in a wagon pulled by mules. Silent black people lined the route, tears streaming down their faces.

Some people at the university had signs in their windows that read "Angela Davis is welcome here." She had been a college professor; now she was a fugitive, sought by the FBI in connection with a terrorist incident.

Two victorious Olympic athletes raised their fists in the Black Power salute during the playing of our national anthem. People wrote to the newspaper and said it was a disgrace. For fifty years, there had been a song known as the "Negro National Anthem":

> *Lift ev'ry voice and sing,*
> *Till earth and heaven ring,*
> *Ring with the harmonies of liberty;*
> *Let our rejoicing rise*
> *High as the list'ning skies,*
> *Let it resound loud as the rolling sea.*

> —"Lift Every Voice and Sing" from the hymnal, *Lift Every Voice and Sing II*

I had never heard it. Didn't know there was such a thing. Funny: I had gotten an A in every American history course I ever took, but somehow I'd missed that.

I had lunch with one of my college professors just before I started seminary. We stood by my car in the parking lot afterward, while I rummaged for my key; he was

· · · · ·

waiting with me until I got safely inside. A white man saw us together and thought we were a couple. He shot us a look of hate and spat on the ground.

Your sister has a head of curly, light brown hair. Your hair is shiny and black. Her skin is pale. Your skin is the color of *café au lait*. Her eyes are light brown. Your eyes flash black fire. Your eyelashes are long and thick and beautiful. The mother of one of your sister's friends told her daughter that you and Rosie must have had different fathers, because you look so different. You have the same father. I wanted to find that mother and tell her that. I wanted to tell her that some things are none of her business. I wanted to tell her that she needed something with which to occupy her mind more profitably. If she had one. I wanted to shame the bejesus out of her.

But I didn't want you to know. I wish you didn't have to know any of these things. Not until you're old enough.

· · · · ·

Murder, She Read

· · · · ·

"HAVE YOU READ THIS ONE?" Brooke pulls a paperback from her backpack and hands it to me. I scan the cover: vaguely familiar title, vaguely familiar author. But then, they're all vaguely familiar. I read at least one a day. On a rest day I might inhale two of them. Once in a while I'll realize, by the time I reach page twelve or thirteen, that I have read this one before. I usually just read on anyway, if I don't have another murder at hand.

"It's about a serial killer."

I love serial killers. Serial killers and corrupt cops. Once I read one in which the serial killer was a corrupt cop. It was heaven. I also love megalomaniacal presidents and ex-KGB agents. I was concerned in the early nineties, as the Cold War fretted to its end—what would we do for espionage novels? I needn't have worried; the Russian *mafya* versus the CIA more than suffices.

Not everyone at St. Clement's knows of my addiction. They may believe that I am too wrapped up in earnest books about church growth and the writings of the Christian mystics to bother with anything as unedifying as a murder mystery. Wrong. I adore murders. On a long afternoon full of interruptions, I daydream of being at home in bed reading one, noticing clues, keeping a mental list of suspects, motives, and alibis in hopes that I will solve the case before the protagonist does. I love long plane rides, the kind everyone else dreads—New York to Arkansas via

· · · · ·

Atlanta with a two-hour layover—because nobody can bother me while I read my murders. I get two or three coffee refills at the corner diner, renting the table so I can finish a chapter in peace. I have chosen a murder over *The New York Times* to read on the train many times, and many times I have read a murder when I really should have been working on my sermon.

Fred calls. Ph.D. from Harvard. Theologian. Understands quantum physics. Probably reads Wittgenstein at the beach. What have I read lately that I might recommend to people? I think hard. Probably I shouldn't name the one I just finished about a busload of deaf children who outwit their murderous kidnapper with the help of a dedicated hostage negotiator. And maybe not the female medical examiner novel I'm finishing today. It has great autopsy descriptions. But Fred is looking for something a little more . . . devotional. I sift through a fair number of titles before I come up with one that doesn't feature a detective and at least one corpse. I recommend a wonderful book about the relationship between monastic vows and Gandhi's philosophy of nonviolence, and settle back down with the medical examiner.

There are many murderously-inclined women operating openly at St. Clement's. We swap murders, waiting impatiently for one another to finish one so that we may pounce on it. I wonder, sometimes, why it might be that these nice Christian women should be so attracted to murder. We all work hard for many good causes. We are all lovers of peace, one supposes, following the Prince of Peace as we do. We all oppose capital punishment. Just about all of us have chosen to serve nonprofit

. . . . .

organizations instead of other places where we could make bunches of money. Good women. But the murder table at St. Clement's spring and fall book sales always groans with our leavings—it's two tables, actually, with more boxes underneath, there are so many murders. Each of us walks away from it like a drunk from a liquor store, a shopping bag filled with murders in each hand. A decent fix for a week or two.

My husband doesn't read murders. He reads obscure eighteenth-century poems, and books about eighteenth-century landscape design. He laughs when he comes upon me reading a murder in bed. We come home on the train together and walk from the station. We go upstairs. I am in bed with a murder before he's finished brushing his teeth.

I think of writing them myself. I think of what characters I might develop. Who might be my protagonist? But I shrink from the autobiographical nature of fiction writing, from what it reveals about the author's inner self, from creating evil characters and giving them words and action, from the doom of their victims, from describing their wounds. People say I should write murders that are set in churches. That's a great idea! All the murders could happen on Saints' Days. A friend offers some really grisly things you could do to a person involving certain articles of church hardware. Can I steal it? No, he says; he's going to use it, a little annuity for his retirement. Oh well, I probably wouldn't have done anything with it anyhow.

The English, I have noticed, content themselves with fewer corpses than the Americans. On average. Our secular archetypes are all there—the fashion model, the

Hollywood agent, the flamboyant tycoon, the heartless movie producer, the burnt-out NYPD detective with one more case left in him before he drinks himself to death. Theirs have more elderly ladies in cardigans than ours, more dead bodies in vicarages, more literary and philosophical musings. We have more guns. Of course. Art imitates life.

But I learn a *lot* from my murders, I protest to my skeptical husband when he asks me, yet again, what exactly I derive from all this literary carnage. I learn things about how the body decomposes and how to deal with someone who is trying to kill you. *Be calm* is the first thing, of course. I imagine myself as a solver of crime, a stopper of crime before it happens, a calm voice in the midst of murderous anger, a saver of the innocent. A heroine. But when, in real life, I was pursued by a stalker and he showed up at the church on Palm Sunday, all of my borrowed law enforcement skills deserted me in an instant. I was so agitated that the policeman answering the call mistook me for my assailant, who stood quiet and calm and mildly interested, as if watching a play. He got into the squad car with great dignity, leaving me apologizing to everyone at the scene for yelling. And when my husband and I were carjacked, I screamed and got out of the car and screamed some more for help and tried to hang onto the door handle as the car pulled away. My absence and the quiet it brought to the situation probably saved Q's life. He was fine, my husband: calm, kind to the carjacker, sympathetic to his semi-coherent story. His wife—the priest—was screaming. The guy let him go after an hour or two, and he was home for dinner. At the trial, he read an eloquent and even tender letter to the

· · · · ·

defendant, begging him to use his prison time to get clean and get his life back. A grace-filled letter his wife—the priest—did not write.

Ah. No wonder I love my murders: they lend me the bravery of others. They lend me their principled goodness. They lend me the courage of their heroes and, for a few hours, I feel what it must be like to be brave. And they lend me rage against their villains, a rage safely removed from any of my shabby angers. I cast myself in the chase and the apprehension of the guilty, in the confrontation between the forces of good and the forces of evil, the decisive vanquishing of the oppressor that never happens in real life. In real life, I am compromised and compromising, biting my tongue and sitting on my hands through the ambiguous days, rerunning my poor choices at night. And so I run for cover into the murder books—into a world in which, in the end, the contrast between good and evil is clear. In which the winners are brave and trust in their own instincts. Braver than I am. Quicker than I am. Surer than I am.

* * *

Just today—just after having written the previous paragraph, in fact—I am walking back to St. Clement's from the publisher's Fifth Avenue offices. I make the turn onto Broadway from 42nd Street and see three people coming toward me. Two women are walking together and talking; a man in a long navy blue coat is behind them. But he is walking too close to them. He is off balance, and too close to the one on the left if he is not walking with them, and I think he is not: they seem

· · · · ·

unaware of his presence. As I pass them I see his arm move, and then I see him reach into the woman's backpack. I wheel and grab his arm.

"Stop!" Everyone turns to look at me. "Ma'am, check your backpack. This man had his hand in your backpack."

The startled woman stares at me and does not move. I've still got the man's arm, and he is recovering. I look around for a cop.

"Take your hands off me! You crazy?" He gives his arm a shake, but I do not release my grip.

"Check your backpack, Ma'am. He was trying to rob you." She does not move, just stands as if rooted to the spot. Her friend is staring at me, too. A man who has stopped to watch turns and walks away.

"I said get off me! Whaddaya doin', bitch?"

"You were robbing her, and you know it. I saw you." He lifts his free arm to strike me, and I let go of his other arm. The women back away.

"Bitch! I din't do nothin'."

"I saw you."

"Bitch! I work." Odd to bring that up at a time like this, but it's what he said.

"I saw you."

The women are still rooted to the spot, and the man starts to run. I look around again. Still no cops. "Watch your bag, Ma'am," I say, and resume my walk.

Two other men pass me. "She didn't check her bag," says one over his shoulder.

"Yeah," I say. "Whatever, right?" This passes for conversation in New York.

. . . . .

Unfinished, my citizen's arrest. Compromised. I didn't receive the stunned thanks of a woman whose wallet didn't get pinched. But I did stop a crime. And a Times Square pickpocket—middle-aged, 5'1", 160 pounds, goatee, salt-and-pepper hair cut short, long coat, glasses—now knows he's not as quick as he used to be.

I didn't nail the bad guy. But, hey. I think I ruined his day.

I HAVEN'T BEEN IN A CHURCH for a week and a half. Here in the south of India it's been Hindu temples, mostly: old ones and new ones, temples with towering fifteenth-century *gopalam*; entry gates teeming with exquisite lacey carvings of their many gods, the gods' consorts, and their animal companions, kings of ancient dynasties, famous holy men, flowers, and mythic beasts. Temples whose priests are distinguished by the long, thin "holy threads" that adorn their bare chests and signify their office, and by the special marks on their foreheads signifying their order. Temples whose *sancta sanctorum* contain the ancient, phallic *lingam* of Shiva, or dancing Shiva, or the jovial elephant face of Ganesh, or the motionless Vishnu reclining on a five-headed cobra. Or a seven-headed one. Or a twelve-headed one. Or a standing Vishnu, austere and mighty. Or Krishna with his flute. In these short weeks I have come to see that "more" is the essential word in Hinduism: nothing is left out, everything is included, the world is burgeoning with sacredness, rendering cows and spices and rivers and trees and stones and suffering . . . holy. There have also been mosques: abstract, intellectual masterworks of the stone carver's art, the call to prayer sounding from their minarets and falling upon the towns in a constant reminder of God that we don't hear much in New York. So devout a society is this that I even saw a *Communist* temple: its outer wall striped red and white like a Hindu temple, but with the hammer and sickle ensconced where the god would ordinarily be. Now *that* would make a Brahmin sweat, I thought, as our bus rumbled past it.

But now we're in a church. It's even my brand, the oldest Anglican church in Asia. Of course, it wasn't *always* ours: the Portuguese built it, the Dutch took it over, and then it had a long run under the British before becoming part of the Church of South India after independence. Vasco da Gama was buried here, although they later dug him up and took him back to Portugal where he came from. Eli Yale was married here, and his son David is buried not far from here; we paid a courtesy call to the tomb, our regret at his early demise tempered by the knowledge that there would be no alumni association to take us to India if the sad event had not left Eli without an heir.

The church is fairly plain, reflecting British restraint more than it does Catholic piety, and so there is not much in the way of paintings and statuary to lift the mind to God. They put up stone tablets inscribed with the Creed, the Lord's Prayer, and the Ten Commandments, just like in the churches of their era at home, filling the sanctuary with such a sober abundance of sober verbiage that it is easy to miss the simple golden cross above the altar. But never mind: it's a church, and that's enough.

I slip into one of the cane-seated pews and sit down. Tourists come and go, examining the pulpit, reviewing the commandments, peeking into the vestry on the side. I gaze at the cross as people cross to and fro in front of it. Nobody would have passed such a cross without reverencing it when this church was built. Of course, there were no tourists when this church was built.

I like to pray with my imagination wide open. I like to imagine lifting people and situations up to a loving God who knows our needs before we ask. But India is heavy and hard to lift. My days here have been too full of its paradoxes to understand them yet, and I am beginning to suspect that I never will. Where should I begin to imagine India? With the elephant who stood near the door of a temple and blessed me on my head with his trunk, having first relieved me of a ten rupee note? Or with children who can smile with real joy and beg at the same time? With a funeral procession making its slow way along a country road toward a black pyre waiting in the middle of a field of fresh green? Perhaps I should pray with the group of young women who rub an ancient statue with fragrant yellow turmeric and circle it three times in a quiet line: "They are praying to God to have children," our guide tells me. Perhaps I should lift *them* in prayer, in their bright saris and complicated jewelry and intense yearning.

But I can't lift all these women. I can't even lift one thin woman, carrying a flat basket of heavy stones on her head. Or a row of women bent double over their tea plants, carefully picking the leaves and putting them gently into the cloth bags they wear on their backs. Actually, the tea plants are not theirs at all. They belong to the plantation owner. Eight or ten hours of this arduous work yields them a hundred rupees—a little less than two dollars. I can't lift *that*.

We had an earthquake here a week ago. Enormous: 7.9 on the Richter scale, they said it was. The front page of *The Hindu* is full of pictures today and has been since it happened: two little boys trying frantically to reach their dead mother, who is lodged firmly beneath a cement slab. A man weeping while his wife's body burns beside him in the ruins of their house, one of her arms raised stiffly upright in the flames, as if in entreaty for rescue. The crushed remains of a school in which forty children and their teacher perished in an instant. Eighteen thousand dead so far. Many more lie beneath the flattened buildings. They'll never know how many, our guide says simply. But I cannot lift all that concrete, all those dead.

There is classical Indian music in the air as we come to a stop at the place where Mohandas Gandhi was assassinated. A museum has been created around the place: photographs of Gandhi as a child, as a barrister, in South Africa as he began to develop and put into practice his philosophy of nonviolent resistance, photographs of him burning imported fabrics, of Gandhi spinning his own cotton, of Gandhi with famous westerners, of his funeral processions through the streets of Delhi, of his flaming funeral pyre, of Nehru standing next to it, the furrows of his sad face even deeper than they usually were. A large room is filled with old-fashioned dioramas, dolls dressed by their maker with great attention to detail, posed in tableaux from the Mahatma's life. There is the room in which Gandhi spent his last days, containing his bed and his worldly goods: a bowl and a cup, a pair of glasses, a notebook, a pen. And from this room issues a path into a garden, the path along which Gandhi walked for the last time; they have installed terracotta "footprints" along the path, so that we imagine his bare feet heading serenely toward death. The killer struck at the path's end. There, with a bullet in his chest, Gandhi bowed to his assassin in the traditional Hindu salute, and blessed him in the name of God.

. . . . .

Gandhi seems not to have been as worried about his own strength and power to do good as I usually am. Perhaps he did things differently. Perhaps he did not feel he *had* to lift all those people and concerns to God, even in his imagination. Perhaps he believed that they were *already* in the presence of God, that God was already present in them. Perhaps he had learned how much energy rebelling against suffering consumes, and the denial of reality it entails. There must have been in him a large measure of what I see in so many people here: they are poor, and they know it. Their lives are determined in many ways by forces outside themselves. But it is nonetheless true that there is palpable joy that lives here much more visibly than the joy we can muster at home. We are outraged about everything, eager to argue, willing to litigate, convinced of our own victimhood, lovingly nursing and brooding over our grievances, large and small. And they, who live on the side of the road in houses made of grass, smile broadly at one another and at us.

I want to say the smiles are happy. They appear so to me, happier than our ironic smiles. And yet the word will not flow from my pen: I don't want to be a rich person professing envy of the primitive spiritual wisdom of the poor, shedding crocodile tears about the contrast between my own dreadful complexity and their charming simplicity. I don't want to play the old you-be-spiritual-and-I'll-be-rich game the West has played with the Third World throughout the century just past. I don't want to romanticize poverty. I don't want to indulge a selfish nostalgia for the rusticity of others. There is no romance in hunger and disease.

Seventy-five per cent of the world's software is now created here, our guide tells us as we drive along the broad and prosperous streets of Bangalore. There have always been a few very rich Indians and many, many very poor ones; there is now a large middle class, growing in number and influence every day. Their billboards scream, as ours do, of movie stars, fast cars, expensive consumer goods. Schools are everywhere: computers, engineering, agriculture, medicine, electronics of all kinds. If only two per cent of all these students are brilliant, I think as we pass the schools, the supply of brilliant people in the world will double. Maybe triple. India is poised to become a very different presence in the world, and this will come to pass in a very short time. Next time you come, says our guide, you will find it completely different here.

I think of the beautiful smiles, the beautiful women in their bright saris, the children walking, in uniform but barefoot, to school; the lush, well-cultivated fields, the people washing clothes in the rivers, the men on bicycles dwarfed by the loads they carry, loads we would carry on dump trucks, the camels pulling carts, the teams of oxen. How will it look, I wonder? Will they lose some of the same things we have lost? Will their smiles become ironic, like ours?

A school of ancient Indian martial arts. We watch the master put his students through their paces: sword fighting in which the opponents seem airborne, combat with spears and daggers, a whip-sword whirring invisibly through the air, too fast and too razor-sharp for any enemy to come anywhere near its orbit. And staves tipped with fire, whirling dangerously around a young woman who is part of the school and does all the things the young men do. The master, it turns out, is her father, and he has taught her his art, against all traditional expectations. I approach her after the demonstration to tell her how surprised and pleased I am to see a woman compete on so equal a footing with the men. She smiles shyly and looks at the ground, before giggling and running off with one of her male colleagues. I can tell that this breakthrough does not seem as momentous to her as it does to me.

The Taj Mahal glows in the sun against an impossibly blue sky. We return to it several times, to see it in different lights. Its beauty has not been over reported. We stand in the window of the palace in which Shah Jahan, its creator, watched its construction for thirty years—under house arrest all that time, imprisoned by his own son. It is a tomb, as everyone knows: Shah Jahan sleeps in it along with his beloved wife, for whom he built it.

Why did his son imprison him? I ask the guide.

Oh, he wanted to be king, he says with a smile.

I run through my mental store of historical patterns: I can't remember too many sons who overthrew fathers. I'm not sure I can place *any*, in fact. Brothers and sisters, oh yes, and many cousins and in-laws, but a son? What a bitter thing that must have been for the aging ruler. But what a redeeming thing to watch through the window as the beautiful marble tomb took shape against the sky!

Redemption. Maybe that is what is palpable here, more so than at home. I was something just this side of a cadaver when I left New York, exhausted, discouraged, spent. For the first week I said little, slept heavily and often—on buses, on planes, as well as in bed at night. It was really my husband's idea to come here: India was a distant enough place to overrule even *my* addiction to work. But I have regained more of my hostage self each day, claiming it from its awful prison of unmet deadlines and the disappointed expectations of others. So much in my life should be other than it is, I think, as we rumble through the countryside in our rickety bus. I imagine that things at home continue much as they were when I left, but they manage to do so without my presence. Whatever is there will still be there when I return, and I suppose I will be able to make some of it better. And some of it will stay the same. And some of it will get worse.

Poor Shah Jahan, looking out the window at his life's work, unable ever to see it up close, to touch the marble or see the precisely-shaped flecks of semiprecious stones glinting in the sun. His plan was to make the tomb a sublime eternal monument to his dead love. Her body would rest in the absolute center of an absolutely symmetrical building. All would be perfectly balanced. He had intended to build a corresponding tomb for himself across the lake from the Taj. It would have been of marble as black as the marble of the Taj is white. The two of them would have faced each other forever, symmetrical, cool. Perfect.

But that was before things went wrong for him. Things always go wrong, I think as I begin to doze in my seat.

So he never built his beautiful black tomb. That particular symmetry was not to be. Now his body lies near hers in the Taj. It is off center in relation to hers. The plan is spoiled. And yet it is that very thing that breathes life into the monument. It is that very flaw which most moves me.

. . . . .

In poetry, my husband has told me, you find God most present in the place where the meter breaks. Here God has a chance to shine unexpectedly. If all goes according to plan, nothing can make us marvel. God, in the disturbing of the symmetry upon which we insist. God, in the possibility of hope amid the ashes.

Yesterday, rescuers unearthed two unexpected survivors of the earthquake: a woman nine months pregnant, who gave birth later in the day. Mother and child are said to be doing fine.

Redemption.

A MEMBER OF THE MAINTENANCE CREW will find them, usually, and will bring them to the attention of the verger, who will place them in a box he keeps in the sacristy for that purpose. Usually it is one bone at a time that has worked its way up to the soft green of the churchyard at the corner of Broadway and Wall Street after three centuries of repose. Perhaps "repose" is not the word best used here: life beneath the surface of the ground is not as uneventful as it seems to us. The ground buckles and shifts. The New York City subway runs under Trinity Church's graveyard, as it did not in the seventeenth century, and it makes the graves and their contents unstable. The lids of the old pine boxes shake loose from their ancient hinges, and the remains of the dead are unceremoniously set free. And some of them make for the light, a femur or a rib breaking through from the darkness into our world.

But O! the poor things—*here* is not as they remembered, and we are not as expected. Instead of familiar people and things—the shopkeepers, the blacksmiths, the crier, the carriages of the rich lurching their way through the muddy streets, they emerge into the midst of immense silver buildings, so tall that one must tilt one's head backwards just to see their tops. Even the church has changed: it is not the tiny brick one they remember. It is much larger, and it is *gothic*, like the churches of the old world they thought they had left behind when they came here. The noise is awful, sounds not found in nature, sounds of metal scraping metal, the wail of sirens monstrous in pitch and monstrous in volume, the thousand growls of a thousand internal combustion engines.

But then, what does all that matter? They are just bones, these visitors from three centuries ago. However long or short were their lives, they are over. There is no place for them among us.

They are placed into the bone box.

But the bone box is *full* of bones, other people's bones, bones of people they did not *know* in life, bones of people they did know and didn't *like*, strangers' bones and the bones of friends. How dreadful, now, to have made that slow upward journey through the dirt only to end up here, in a box on a shelf! And after a time, when the box is full, the verger will call a priest over from across the street, who will reinter the box of unrelated bones.

"You are dust," the priest will say for a second time, "and to dust you will return."

Dark, again. Cold, again. The bones settle into the common bone box. The subway train rumbles through and screams to a halt at Rector Street. And the bones shake a little.

* * *

Seven or eight blocks north lie other bones. These were never archived, as were the bones in Trinity's graveyard. They lived separately from the people of Trinity, although many of them may have worked as their servants; in death, they are also separate, buried outside the wall that gave a famous street its name. They face east, these skeletons, and the buttons are all that remain of their clothing, tin and even gold glinting against the ivory of their ribs. Perhaps it was livery; the best clothing these people had may have been the uniforms provided by their employers.

This is the Negro Burying Ground. Some slaves, more freedmen, they slept in peace for three centuries before the government broke ground for an enormous new office building here in the mid-nineties. Things were different by then. There were many African Americans in suits in the office buildings of the financial district. Turning the Negro Burying Ground and its citizens under like so much compost was not going to fly. The work on the office building stopped.

Respect must be paid to the dead. Those who slept in the Negro Burying Ground had been desecrated long before they ever lay down here—uprooted, taken by force from their African homes, renamed in a guttural, new tongue far removed from their old African speech. Having to buy their freedom from their owners. They deserved to lie undisturbed, finally, after lives so profoundly affected by other people's doings. It was not they who made their way up to the surface, like the white folks buried down the street at Trinity. They did not approach *us*. They stayed still, in their graves, far beneath the pavement, facing east: toward the sun, but also toward home.

The legal proceedings that settled the fate of the Negro Burying Ground took several years. A solution was reached that permitted the office building project to continue, near the Burying Ground but not right down through it. The people will

· · · · ·

stay put, held in their place as before, again by the edifices of the powerful, in death as in life.

They probably worshiped at Trinity, the verger says, together with their masters. The first Trinity Church had separate boxes for seating stable servants, house servants. One young cleric became deeply involved in teaching servants' young children to read. The vestry's reaction seems to have been mixed: some of them, at least, could see where such a thing might lead. But he continued, visiting at night in their quarters, bringing his Bibles and his spellers. At least some of these servants were slaves—more in the seventeenth century than in the eighteenth, fewer in the nineteenth. Then, as now, New York was all about money: the earnestness of the young minister was seconded by an economy that could make more use of wage earners than of slaves, and the city became a magnet for those who had bought their freedom. It would be too much to say that these freedmen lived lives unfettered by oppression—every day of their lives must have carried stern reminders of who they were and, more importantly, who they were *not*—but their New York was becoming a place where their power was awakening and making itself felt.

But still, the longing! The longing of those wives and children, carefully turning the dear dead faces toward Africa before covering them over forever. No wonder those bones did not inch their way up to the surface, like the bones at Trinity. It would not have been enough. Why return to life, a life of freedom so carefully rationed? If it was not to be in Africa, eternity might just as well be spent in the black earth right here. They stayed put, lying very still.

. . . . .

And a grandson became mayor. And a granddaughter became Borough President. And many grandchildren buy and sell in the place where their ancestors were bought and sold. On that street named for the city wall, outside which their forbears had lain down and faced east.